For the Sake of the Bride

For the Sake of the Bride

Restoring the Church to Her Intended Beauty

Second Edition

Steve Harper

Abingdon Press

Nashville

FOR THE SAKE OF THE BRIDE:
RESTORING THE CHURCH TO HER INTENDED BEAUTY

Second edition copyright © 2014 by Abingdon Press

All rights reserved.

This book is printed on acid-free paper.

Library of Congress Cataloging-in-Publication Data has been requested.

ISBN 978-1-63088-570-0

Scripture quotations unless noted otherwise by are from the Common English Bible®. Copyright ©2011 by the Common English Bible. All rights reserved. Used by permission. www.CommonEnglish Bible.com.

Scripture quotations marked (*THE MESSAGE*) are taken from *THE MESSAGE*. Copyright © by Eugene H. Peterson 1993, 1994, 1995, 1996, 2000, 2001, 2002. Used by permission of NavPress Publishing Group.

Scripture quotations marked (KJV) are taken from The Authorized (King James) Version. Rights in the Authorized Version in the United Kingdom are vested in the Crown. Reproduced by permission of the Crown's patentee, Cambridge University Press.

Cover Photo by Jeannie Harper

14 15 16 17 18 19 20 21 22 23—10 9 8 7 6 5 4 3 2 1
MANUFACTURED IN THE UNITED STATES OF AMERICA

Praise for *For the Sake of the Bride*

"Steve Harper writes as an evangelical who loves The United Methodist Church. He has written a thoughtful, helpful, and surprising book on the church he loves and the ways it might wrestle with the issues that divide it."

—*Rev. Adam Hamilton, United Methodist Church of the Resurrection, Leawood, Kansas*

"*For the Sake of the Bride* sets aside the all-too-easy rhetoric of division and antagonism and invites the divided church to fully engage the greater way of love that Jesus models and bids us follow. Harper writes with pastoral courage, sensitivity and genuine humility, inviting us not to a particular position, but to generous dialogue on behalf of the church we cherish."

—*Dr. Kandace Brooks, Senior Pastor, Tamoka United Methodist Church, Ormond Beach, Florida*

"Steve Harper succeeds in his desire to move the Church beyond the impasse of name calling and shouting and calls for schism, and brings us to the table, the Round Table, in a spirit of grace filled love, integrity, honesty and mutual respect for all parties. That's a difficult place for many to maintain, but it's where we all must meet."

—*Dr. Dan Johnson, Senior Pastor, Trinity United Methodist Church, Gainesville, Florida*

"I recommend this book to any and all who seek a way forward from the divisiveness which has shattered the church's witness in a changing world. The highlight of the book for me is its radical humility and its steadfast integrity in maintaining the historic witness to God's way as the way of radical love."

—*William Daylong, Senior Pastor, The United Methodist Church of Mt. Vernon, Iowa*

"Steve Harper offers the Church a road map towards unity and healing among heterosexual and homosexual Christians. He invites all to sit at God's round table where together we prayerfully view God's creative gift of sexual orientations. A place where we can view and grow into the abundant life that God offers in the gift of sexuality."

—*Deen Thompson, Reconciling United Methodist layman*

"Dr. Harper is one of the most respected United Methodist evangelicals. His book will surprise many and even shock some. Yet this wise reflection, bringing a Wesleyan hermeneutic of love and grace to the denominational debate over homosexuality, may be just what we've needed. I hope it is a 'game changer.' I for one plan to 'stay at the table.'"

> —*John Powers, Superintendent, Gulf Central District of the Florida Conference of The United Methodist Church*

"Steve Harper reflects the evangelical and holiness traditions of American Methodists. From this framework of traditional Christian piety, he shows how we can reflect faithfully on these contemporary issues in ways that honor each other as the presence of Christ, the 'bride of Christ.' This is a breath of fresh air amid the rancor that has too often polluted church conversations in recent years. His concern is that Christians damage the church—not just the institution of the church but the church as the body and 'bride of Christ'—by the uncharitable and unprofitable conversation we too often carry on, especially over the issue of same-sex relationships."

> —*Ted Campbell, associate professor of church history, Perkins School of Theology*

"I have many friends from both sides of the (sad) divide over same-sex relationships, but I must say that Steve Harper is about the only one who approaches this matter with nary an angry and militant stance but with the strong, hopeful sense of the third way and the powerful purpose of Love."

> —*Mary Ling, licensed pastor from Singapore*

"*For the Sake of the Bride* is a helpful reflection on the unity of the church concerning human sexuality. He risks moving deeply into the conversation, and he does so in a way that is evangelical (Christocentric) and mystical. His rediscovery of E. Stanley Jones's round-table discussion points a way beyond our tribalism. I hope you will read this book, for the sake of the bride—the church of Jesus Christ."

> —*Bishop Kenneth Carter, the Florida Annual Conference, The United Methodist Church*

"Steve Harper is a longtime mentor and friend; when he says something, I listen. Here he asks Christians to approach tough questions first and foremost in a spirit of unity and holy love. This book will challenge you to respect the other, whichever side of the debate you claim."

> —*Jennifer Woodruff Tait, PhD, managing editor of* Christian History Magazine

Contents

Foreword

Steve Harper's words remind me of an eighteenth-century hymn by William Cowper (1731–1800):

Sometimes a light surprises
　　The Christian while he sings;
It is the Lord who rises
　　With healing in His wings;
When comforts are declining,
　　He grants the soul again
A season of clear shining,
　　To cheer it after rain.

Steve Harper's witness to the work of God's Spirit while in prayer during Lent came as a surprising light breaking through the dark shadows of a deeply conflicted denomination. It offers a healing word for the heartsickness of division that has infected many denominations and especially "the people called Methodists."

Like Cowper's hymn, this book emerges from the broken heart of a faithful disciple who has proven himself to be biblically grounded in his scholarship, unwaveringly orthodox in his faith, profoundly Wesleyan in his theology, and passionately evangelical in his desire to draw people to Jesus Christ. Everyone who knows him knows that Steve Harper's life is deeply rooted in the discipline of prayer.

This book is not an academic treatise or a social manifesto. It is a heartfelt invitation to enter into conversation about same-sex relationships in a way that is centered in the love of God in Christ. The book is, in fact, a very Wesleyan way that may bring healing to some of our painful polarization on this subject.

Steve Harper reminds us of E. Stanley Jones, who modeled a way of being faithful to Jesus Christ while being open to conversation with people who are radically different in their beliefs or convictions. Steve Harper offers a fresh way of hearing the biblical word regarding marriage in general and same-sex relationships in particular—which will be a surprise to some readers and will be rejected by others. It will not satisfy people on the polar opposite ends of the debate, but it will be a welcome word to faithful Christians who are unwilling to divide the church over issues that are not central to our faith and mission.

Steve Harper loves the church and writes with a broken heart. He invites us to join him in loving the church the way God loves it, because God's Son gave his life for it. Steve Harper's words come as a surprising light that carries healing in its wings.

James A. Harnish

Introduction

The season of Lent in 2014 was a turning point for me. I experienced the dying/rising process in a new way as the forty-day period progressed. I entered Lent on Ash Wednesday as one kind of person; I emerged from it at Easter dawn as another kind of person. The rest of this book is my attempt to describe this transformation, and to tell you why it was so important for me to be changed.

During the season of Lent in 2014, the debate over same-gender relationships reignited in the Body of Christ in general and in my own United Methodist Church in particular. The flame of debate has been burning for more than forty years, but in the spring of 2014, it exploded with a new level of heat and destructiveness. The traditional sides engaged in a demeaning point/counterpoint conflict, a tug-of-war, leaving many casualties along the way. Discussions turned derogatory. Unchristian attitudes and actions were exhibited by leaders who should know better, and by those who used social media to throw in their two-cents' worth via what seemed to be a never-ending spate of comments.

All of this was justified—by both sides—because there was "something essential at stake." The battles congealed into an all-out war, which each side was determined it had to win. As one who was just beginning my ordained ministry in The United Methodist Church when the controversy began in 1972, some of the rhetoric and logic was familiar. The pro/con arguments were largely warmed-over versions of longstanding positions.

But in the spring of 2014, I saw a darker picture emerging—a contentiousness between professing Christians and a persecution of the LGBT community by professing Christians. In the season of Lent, the Holy Spirit broke my heart one morning by speaking into it these words: "My Bride, the Church, is being abused. Her gown is being torn to shreds by siblings who are trying to end up with the biggest piece of the cloth, and who would rather expose her nakedness than give up the fight. Enough is enough!"

I was stunned—so much so that I kept the experience to myself. I'm old enough to know the difference between a passing feeling and a sacred impression. Whatever I was feeling needed more time to ponder and to test. Shortly after this, I found my wife, Jeannie, having her own similar, painful experience—along with some of her friends. Soon this rippled out to include many of the men and women whose thoughts I follow and whose witness I respect. As this was happening, I heard the inner voice say, "Are you getting this? Are you realizing that I am raising up a new generation of believers to restore the Bride's intended beauty and to renew her witness? And do you now believe that I want you to be one of the people involved in this?"

Added to the current moment was an earlier decision to re-read the writings of E. Stanley Jones, the person whom overall I consider to have been my primary mentor in things pertaining to theology and Christian living. When I began my re-reading of him, I had no idea that this would merge with my Lenten experience. But it has. And that will become clearer as the book unfolds.

So here I am, convinced that I must try to put into words what has largely been beyond words for some months now. It still is, and that is why I must tell you that while this book is not timid, neither is it terminal. I have come out of Lent 2014 with my boat on a stream that is flowing, not standing still. With each of my previous books, I have had after-publication thoughts, because I have never viewed my writing as a final word. I am even more convinced that this is the case with this book. In the course of writing it I have gone back to re-word and re-express parts of it, because the landscape keeps changing.

But at some point I have come to see that I cannot wait indefinitely to capture the thoughts and feelings that now are transforming my beliefs about the Church and its witness to the world. A work in progress (which is all any writing can be) is better than silence. But I must offer it to you with great humility.

Because the book requires some space to unfold, I must plead with you not to pass judgment until you have read the whole thing. Do not let one sentence, paragraph, or chapter force you to make a conclusion before I have even made one myself. The abuse of the Bride through the culture war about same-gender relationships, as well as a host of other things, cannot be briefly described, much less interpreted. So I ask you to be patient at least to hear the points I am trying to make in their entirety. After that, you must decide what you think about all this, and where you wish to stand relative to it.

As you will shortly see, I am doing my best to write as both one who has been part of the culture war in the past, and as one who has decided not to be part of it in the future. I am writing both as a previous agitator, and hopefully, as a future apologist for a new and better way—a way that will take our abused Bride and make her what God intends for her to be.

In trying to find and navigate this new way, I may end up losing friends on both sides of the traditional debate. But that is a risk I must take. However falteringly, I must make the attempt—for the sake of the Bride.

Steve Harper

One

Let Us Pray

If there were some way to prove it, I would not be surprised to learn that every significant movement of the Spirit has been preceded by prayer. We can see it in the lives of men and women in the First Testament. In the Second Testament, it shows up clearly in Jesus' preparation for his ministry, as well as in the preparation for the birth of the Church on the Day of Pentecost. My study of the Wesleyan tradition further evidences that the prayers of John and Charles Wesley (and other early Methodist people) were frequently doorways into insight and action. All this is another way of saying that God always speaks the first word. Our calling is to listen and to obey.

And so it was for me in the season of Lent in 2014. The transformation God wanted to work in my life began in the prayer closet. So I must begin this book by taking you into that closet in order to show you how my heart was both broken and put back together as a new picture of the Bride of Christ was given me. It came to have the shape of lament—that is, a grieving for the past and a concern for the present, all couched in a hope for the future. In the prayer closet, God gave me pain and promise. A new vision began to emerge—a vision that I barely can describe, and one that I know is larger than my attempt to describe it in this book.

For some time now, I have been using liturgical or public prayer as the basis for my private daily prayers. The words of such prayers serve as windows

1

through which I can look to express my own thoughts and feelings—sometimes in the literal words of the written prayers, but often in expanded and spontaneous expressions that the written words ignite. And that is how my lament for the Bride began. The transformation commenced as I prayed the following prayer from *The Book of Common Prayer*:

> O God the Father of our Lord Jesus Christ, our only Savior, the Prince of Peace: Give us grace seriously to lay to heart the great dangers we are in by our unhappy divisions; take away all hatred and prejudice, and whatever else may hinder us from godly union and concord; that, as there is but one Body and one Spirit, one hope of our calling, one Lord, one Faith, one Baptism, one God and Father of us all, so we may be all of one heart and of one soul, united in one holy bond of truth and peace, of faith and charity, and may with one mind and on mouth glorify thee; through Jesus Christ our Lord, Amen.[1]

With a severe mercy I did not expect, the words of this prayer burned into my soul, almost as if I had never prayed them before. I was awestruck, as I went back over the prayer a number of times and found myself increasingly convicted by both what I read and by what I was experiencing as phrase after phrase opened windows in my whole being to an even wider terrain. I was left, like Job, with my hand over my mouth, unable to speak.

I cannot expect you to have the same response that I had when I prayed this prayer, but if you want to take a few moments to ponder it before you read on, that would be fine. Perhaps it might help you enter into the substance and spirit of the prayer. But whatever you do, please know that it was like a bolt of holy lightning.

Words and phrases such as "seriously to lay to heart the great dangers we are in by our unhappy divisions" branded themselves into my heart. Oh, I had prayed these words, or words like them, many times before. But now...on that day...I realized that I was *praying* them for the first time. I saw that I had not "seriously laid to heart" what the prayer was describing. I had not seen the divisions in the Church as "great dangers"—dangers created precisely by "all hatred and prejudice, and whatever else may hinder us from godly union and concord."

---

1. *The Book of Common Prayer* (New York: Church Publishing Incorporated, 2006), 818.

In a moment of undeniable revelation, I saw that, up to that moment, I had been part of the problem, rather than part of the solution. I had abused the Bride, either by my active participation in the conflict, or (more recently) in my silence in the face of it. The words of the prayer brought all that to an end. I was being called to re-enter the matter—not just the debate about same-gender relationships but also the larger abuses of the Bride, brought on largely by sibling believers. But I also knew that I was being called to re-enter it in a new way.

Like Velcro, the words of this prayer sealed themselves onto my whole being, so that other prayers from *The Book of Common Prayer* began to stick and exert their influence. Here are just a few examples, but as you will know, the *prayerbook* is filled with many other similar prayers:

> For the welfare of the holy Church of God, and for the unity of all peoples. (p. 383)

> Father, we pray for your holy catholic Church, that we all may be one. (p. 387)

> Grant, Almighty God, that all who confess your Name may be united in your truth, live together in your love, and reveal your glory in the world. (p. 388)

> For the holy Church of God, that it may be filled with truth and love, and be found without fault at the day of your coming, we pray to you, O Lord. (p. 389)

> For the peace and unity of the Church of God. (p. 392)

The Holy Spirit was now in my face asking without reservation, "Do you believe these prayers? If so, why are you not acting like it?" I could no longer deny that the Bride was being abused, by members of her own family, and that I was a contributing party to the abuse. I began to pray for forgiveness, and for grace to be given a vision for a way to help restore honor to the Bride, and the will to carry it out.

I find myself in this chapter at the place of saying something I will say more than once in the course of this book: I am not asking you to have the same response to these prayers that I had, and I am not going to use my experience to create another wall of division between myself and anyone else. But like the apostles of old, I cannot keep from telling you what I have seen and heard (Acts 4:20). And what I saw and heard during Lent 2014 has changed the way I view all the controversies we are facing in the Body of Christ. It has changed the way I view the debate about same-gender relationships. This book is a recounting of the new sights and sounds that have emerged—for the sake of the Bride.

Two

The Weeping Trinity

When God began to break my heart about these things, I saw that God's heart was broken too. Realizing that my attitudes and actions, no matter how sincere, had brought shame upon the Bride left me with nothing else to say except, "Lord, have mercy! Christ, have mercy!" For the first time, I realized that as one ordained to keep truth and love connected—as one ordained to maintain the unity of the Church in the bond of love—as one ordained to promote the welfare of the Body of Christ, I had both knowingly and unknowingly contributed to the turmoil. Without ever intending to, I had been one of those abusing the Bride.

Let me hasten to tell you that I am not fixated on the Church in this book. I grieve for those peoples and groups that the Church (the naked Bride) has hurt with her words and deeds. And there are plenty of them—human beings who have suffered collateral damage from our religious and cultural warfare. My lament includes them. But the new thing I saw during Lent 2014 was the shame we Christians have brought on the Bride.

Moreover, I take seriously St. Peter's words that judgment begins within God's house (1 Peter 4:17), and I now believe that if the Church's witness is to be credible, we must first get our house in order. We have spent far too much time looking over the fence into the yards of others (including the yards of fellow Christians), and far too little time seeing the weeds in our own.

The Holy Spirit's exhortation, "Enough is enough," included the clear call to become spiritually near-sighted for a season, so that a spirit of confession and repentance might take the place of condemnation and degradation. I saw the Trinity weeping.

The Father of the Bride weeps because the Church (as the new Israel) is supposed to be a light to the nations. The Bride is in the world to reveal the wonder and beauty of God. Instead of this, we have given the impression that God is angry with the world, and in a disposition of condemnation, when the opposite is true (see John 3:16-17). The Church was given to the world to show how human beings are meant to live when they are under the influence of God's grace. Instead, we have been brothers and sisters who cannot and will not get along. The Father who made us weeps.

The Bridegroom (the Son) weeps because the Church is laid bare, looking more like a grotesque caricature than his dearly loved Bride. In our sibling tug-of-war, we have treated fellow Christians and others in the world with less charity than pagans give to each other. When Jesus asked if he would find faith on the earth when he returned, I took that to mean that the increase of evil would, like a bad weed, come near to choking out the crop. Now, I have added to my list of possibilities that the Church may so misrepresent the gospel that the world would not touch Christianity with a ten-foot pole. The Son knows how beautiful his Bride is, so he weeps when we distort her image in the world, leaving people to reject what ends up being only a counterfeit version of the Bride.

The Friend of the Bridegroom (Holy Spirit) weeps because the Church is meant to bear the fruit of the union of the Son and the Bride: love, joy, peace, patience, kindness, goodness, faithfulness, gentleness, and self-control (Gal 5:22-23). Instead, we offer the waxed fruit of hatred, sour godliness, strife, impatience, harshness, compromised character, roughness, infidelity, and a life out of control. Jesus said that we would be known by our fruit, and the seeds of our un-Christlikeness are now manifesting themselves in ways that bring shame to the Bride.

When I saw the Trinity weeping, I wondered why I had never wept for the Church during all these long years of controversy. Why had I joined the ranks of those who would rather win than weep? How had this happened—

when I had been praying the kinds of prayers I described in the last chapter? How had this happened when, first as a member, I vowed to uphold the Church by my prayers, presence, gifts, and service—and then subsequently vowed to be a clergyperson who would honor the Bride.

Lent 2014 was a hard time for me—a time when I was being turned every which way but loose. But after accepting the reality and the necessity of what was happening, I began to feel that all this was for good (Rom 8:28), if I were willing to stay strapped into the roller-coaster seat and ride it out to the end of the line. It is a journey I am compelled to make—for the sake of the Bride.

Three

No More Sides

Early in my experience I saw more clearly than ever before that Jesus was able to make friends with people who were unable to make friends with each other. I saw that this was a deliberate choice on his part—another way of revealing what life in the kingdom is supposed to look like. I also saw that this approach caused him to lose friends who were righteous or who were sinners.

In short, I saw the inability of dualistic thinking to take us where we need to go in restoring intended honor to the Bride. I saw that dualistic thinking (while necessary for making legitimate comparisons and fostering appropriate differentiation) too easily leads to either/or thinking—which leads quickly to a hierarchical way of thinking. In the "good, better, best" world, egotism (the fallen self) quickly *assumes* superiority over a person or group. We pray the prayer of the Pharisee, "God, I thank you that I am not like other people," when in fact we are exactly like other people. We are all sinners. There is no righteous person, not even one. Not even one.

But taking sides and ascribing superiority to one side or the other (actually both sides claim the higher ground, and that's what leads to the derogatory interaction), only creates a downward spiral where one group vilifies the other group—and in the case of differences between Christians, we make sure we do this "in the name of Jesus."

While re-reading E. Stanley Jones, *Growing Spirituality*, my emerging vision clarified even more. Referring to St. Paul, he wrote:

The Greatest Christian said, "I am controlled by the love of Christ." This cuts deep. It is possible to be controlled by the love of achievement, of success, of a cause, of one's fight. To be controlled by the love of Christ is different not only in degree but also in kind, in quality.[1]

Jones did not write these words from the ivory tower. Rather, he wrote them nearly fifty years after he first set foot in India and saw the sides that were dividing religions, the Christian church, and the state. In fact, he saw them while sailing to India, observing prejudice as caste and class had divided India into multiple factions. From the outset he realized that he could not be on any side but rather had to pray for a new way to minister. I will write about this in more detail later in the chapter entitled, "Gathering at the Round Table."

When I read Jones's observation, I was again cut to the heart. The words, "it is possible to be controlled by...a cause, or one's fight," branded themselves into my whole being. Like never before, I saw that this is what has happened in the debate about same-gender relationships, and it is what happens in almost every manifestation of factionalism. But I also saw E. Stanley Jones as a solid Christian who never stopped believing there was a better way. And by grace, he found it. And once he found it, he made it a mainstay in his life, his relationships, and his ministry.

Reading Jones afresh took me immediately to the ministry of Martin Luther King, Jr. As he watched the hatred between the races escalate, he too realized that he could not be on a side. Neither the Black Panthers nor the Ku Klux Klan held the key to the future, even though each group claimed they did.[2] King found his better way when he read E. Stanley Jones' biography of Gandhi, writing in the margin of the cover page, "This is it!" And from that

---

1. E. Stanley Jones, *Growing Spirituality* (New York: Pierce & Washabaugh, 1953), 124.

2. I realize that both in Jones's situation in India and in King's dilemma here in the United States there were more than two "sides." But it is not my purpose to do a social analysis. Instead, I want to make the point that these leaders refused to take a "side," choosing to pray and to work for another way forward. This is a choice that I have made, and one I am trying to describe in this book.

day forward, he embedded his portion of the civil-rights movement in non-violence, often referring to it as "the strength to love."

Although it is beyond the scope and purpose of this book, once I realized there were people who had influenced me significantly, who had abandoned the approach of choosing sides and found another way forward, I began to recall many other women and men in history—ancient and modern—who gave up dualistic thinking and the either/or, right/wrong debates that arise from it.

My experience in Lent 2014 absolutely convinced me that in the debate about same-gender relationships (and other divisive issues that we face), we have reached a time when no side can take us where we need to go. The time for pejorative attitudes and polarizing actions is over—or at least it should be. As clearly as I have ever heard the Spirit speak, I heard these words in my soul, "No more sides"—for the sake of the Bride.

Four

A Third Way

When I pondered the examples of Jones and King, I saw that they, and others like them, were able to rise above dualistic thinking and find a third way through the challenges they faced. I am on a journey to do the same with the divisive issues we face in the Church and society today. Dualistic thinking that goes to excess must be challenged and laid aside if we are to make progress in fulfilling our mission of making disciples.

In the beginning, dualistic thinking is necessary. It is the way we know things by comparison and contrast. An airplane is like a bird. A wheel is like a tire. A tree is not a ball. A car is not a sunset. Dualistic thinking rightly recognizes differentiation. And there is nothing in this book that attempts to ignore legitimate differences. The issue is *how* we deal with our differences. And that's why dualistic thinking cannot take us where we need to go. Instead of helping us, it creates a downward spiral that makes things worse rather than better.

Differentiation deteriorates into divisiveness. Divisiveness moves into declaration ("my side is the right side"), which only produces defensiveness on the part of those who have now been declared to be wrong. At this stage, the opposite side reacts and claims to be right. The contest is underway. When the sides are both right, the only way to appear to be the true right, is to degrade the other side. Caricatures and clichés emerge, often trumping content. The process goes into destructiveness, where winning is the goal—and always "for the sake of the cause."

Dualistic thinking pervades nearly every part of our lives, especially evident in advertising, which reinforces the "good, better, best" mentality and which (even if kindly) tells us that one product is superior to another. Dualistic thinking not only tempts us; it trains us to use the same tactics when we deal with people, places, and things. Almost without even realizing it, we are conditioned to enter into life not simply differentiating but dividing and conquering.

To come out of this process requires insight and courage. The insight is fundamentally that those who choose a third way will not be welcomed by either of the sides. And because we like to be liked—by somebody, anybody—we gravitate toward a side rather than calling the process of taking sides into question. Jesus challenged the status quo when he told his disciples not to trust the yeast of the Sadducees or the Pharisees (Matt 16:5). Neither side had the complete picture. The whole ministry of Jesus was a third way, and we will return to that in the chapter, "The Son's Photograph."

E. Stanley Jones saw this in India when people were converted to Christianity from other religions. When one such person became a Christian, the Christians did not trust him (thinking he might be a spy in the camp), and the religion from which he had come now considered him a traitor. Seeing this happen over and over, Jones became convinced that the third way was not to create sides between Christians and those of other faiths, but rather to lift up Christ, the One in whom God's synthesis occurs. He based his whole ministry on three words: "Jesus is Lord," and refused to make any other factor primary.

If I am able, I hope to show that a similar synthesis "in Christ" is possible as we face divisive issues in general, and as we debate same-gender relationships in particular. The very nature of the third-way enterprise will be limited and incomplete, because we do not often see it attempted. We do not see it fully applied in the divisive issues of our day. And when we do, it is often caricatured as inadequate by the dualistic thinkers who must have it one way or the other. An invitation to a third way is actually more difficult than choosing a side and then defending it to the death. But I am convinced that we must move beyond dualistic thinking and give third-way thinking a try.

I am encouraged to do this by my own Wesleyan tradition. John and Charles Wesley were adept at merging theology and practice in a both/and fashion, rather than an either/or one. In fact, the Methodist movement can be viewed as a third-way enterprise, finding a way to synthesize the parachurch and the Church. And like others who made similar attempts before them, the Wesleys found themselves caught between the side who believed the Church was the be-all-and-end-all, and the side that believed the Church was bankrupt and that true spirituality could only be found outside it. But John and Charles, along with those who joined their effort, persevered in the belief that a union of *ecclesia* and *ecclesiola* was possible.[1] And they chose to make their synthesis a movement rooted in the love of God—for the sake of the Bride.

---

1. These words describe the Church (*ecclesia*) and what we today call the parachurch (*ecclesiola*), with the belief that the "little church" was meant to be within the "big Church"—often as a renewal agent within it.

Five

The Way of Love

By naming the restoration of the Bride as the way of love, I am not trying to insinuate but rather to inspire. I realize there are people who have taken their sides because they love the Church, but when the choice becomes a tug-of-war that shreds the fabric of the Bride's gown, love has been set aside in favor of something else, whatever it happens to be. The Apostle Paul clearly says that love is "the better way" (1 Cor 12:31). This being so, we must return to it as the basis for our future in the Body of Christ.

I think of this in the way I think of a making a cake. We start with the ingredients, and then combine them in ways that produce an actual cake. For us Christians, the key ingredient is love. We mix it with other things (some of which I will describe in upcoming chapters), allowing the ingredients to blend and to bake. By the grace of God, we end up with an ecclesial cake flavored and decorated to suit the context and the circumstances that gave rise to it in the first place.

To choose the way of love as the defining phrase for the restoration of the Bride calls us to realize that love is indeed a many-splendored thing. To call love the key ingredient is to understand that it is itself made up of a constellation of factors. The purpose of this chapter is to describe some of them, so that when we move into other important elements of the restorative process, we will be doing so as those who have made "the better way" our way.

First of all, the way of love is the way of *agapē*. When Paul wrote that he was controlled by the love of God, he used this word. And when he commended the way of love in his first letter to the Corinthians, he used the same word to describe the kind of love that we are to embrace and express.

The word *agapē* was a rare word compared to the other three words for love in the Greek language. Biblical scholars believe that the early Christians chose the word as a way of saying to the culture that the kind of love being described was different from the other kinds of love with which it was familiar.[1] The early Christians were saying that there was something more to the life of love than the customary words could describe, either individually or when taken together—something essentially holy and of God.

The fundamental difference lies in the fact that *agapē* puts the impulse to love in the nature of the lover, rather than in the nature of the one loved. In other words, *agapē* is the kind of love that is given because of *who* the lover is, not who the loved one is. It is love given without any consideration of the person being loved. And that is why it seemed to be so radical—and when we stop to ponder it today, it is as challenging as ever. We have a world that says, "I will love you, if I think you are lovable. I will love you as long as you respond to my love. I will love you as long as I think you merit my love." *Agapē* is not like that. It does not operate that way.

Early Christians used this word to describe God's love. There was no human being who could love this way naturally, universally, and indefinitely. Only God could do this, and *agapē* means that this is exactly what God does—for everyone, everywhere, all the time. But they did not stop there. They went on to assert that God could put this love into human beings, and that we could love others the way God loves us. In fact, they said, this has happened because God's love spreads through Christ, spreads into our hearts, and changes our lives.

This is the most radical thought ever to be put on the table of human consideration. The world had previously seen good people and great people, but when Jesus came, the world saw "*Agapē* Man." His incarnation drew a line across time, marking the beginning of "a new creation," a creation by Christ, with Christ, in Christ, and for Christ. His redemption bought us back

---

1. William Barclay, *New Testament Words* (London: SCM Press, 1964), 17–30. Barclay provides a good overview for all the Greek words for love: *erōs, storgē, phileo,* and *agapē.*

from the rejection of God's love, or even the minimizing of it, to an abundant life whose center reference point was *agapē*.

This is where the way of love begins for us. We are no less amazed or challenged by this revelation. The issue is not revelation but rather reception. The issue is not the acknowledgment of *agapē* but the application of it—without qualification of any kind. If nothing can separate us from the love of God in Christ Jesus (Rom 8:38-39), then nothing must separate us from expressing the love of God in Christ Jesus—nothing.

The whole Christian life is predicated on love—what Jesus named as the two great commandments: loving God and loving others, plain and simple. The challenge for me was to de-contaminate my theology of love; that is, to cleanse it of the other ways I had come to qualify, limit, and define it. I saw more clearly than ever that I was being asked to lay aside all my conditioned justifications for not fully living the two great commandments.

The most frightening and startling thing that has happened to me in decades is to be left with nothing but love. What in the world am I to do with that? This book will not and cannot answer that question, because the only way to "work out what God has worked in"[2] is to spend the rest of my life applying *agapē* to all of my life. I am under no illusion that making this attempt will mean perfect performance. I am still liable to the same misplaced attitudes and actions. But something radical has changed, and I must bear witness to it: the way of love is now the "north star" by which I am being called to navigate my life. Will I always get it right? Will any of us? No. But with the way of love as the center, we not only redraw the circumference but we also have a way of telling when we depart from it. As Charles Wesley wrote, "If to the right or left I stray, that moment, Lord, reprove."[3]

This means secondly that the way of love is the way of humility. When the Wesleys were asked to name the evidence of perfect love, they drew upon the witness of the Christian tradition and rightly called it humility. This is, and always was supposed to have been, the mark of love. Humility can be described in many ways, but for now, let's simply say it is the ability to live a

---

2. A phrase that Oswald Chambers used to describe how the love of God becomes incarnate in us.

3. A phrase from his hymn, "I Want a Principle Within." And for him, it was the principle of love.

life that does not become judge and jury over anyone else. It is the God-given ability to hold convictions without turning them into hammers to smash those who look at life differently than we do.

When dualistic thinking becomes toxic, it turns relationships into hierarchies. When this happens, egotism seizes upon an alleged superiority, which even if correct to a point, nevertheless poisons the relationship from then on. Humility, on the other hand, keeps the relationship flat (rather than hierarchical), so that a genuine conversation can continue. Without humility, conversations erode into point/counterpoint arguments, with the ever-increasing need to win. And for these kinds of reasons, our predecessors in the faith have held themselves accountable to the way of love by identifying it through the behavior of humility.

The third factor in the way of love is non-judgment. This is so important that I will return to it in the chapter, "The Witness of Tradition." But for now, it is our commitment not to degrade or vilify another person—no matter what. As we will see, this sentiment is illustrated by Jesus, Paul, and the Christians who came after them. It is now handed to us.

Among other things, non-judgment means we will not talk about people without also talking with them. It means we will not set up a straw man, comparing the best of our position with the worst of someone else's. It means we will not reach conclusions without allowing those convictions to be shaped by community—community in which all parties are allowed to speak to and to shape the future. Very simply, non-judgment means keeping some things to yourself, so that another person can have time and space to live. Love does not rejoice in wrongdoing (1 Cor 13:6)—including the evil of demeaning another person who is made in the same image of God that we are.

Fourthly, the way of love means the way of fair comparison. I alluded to this in the previous paragraph, but I want to highlight it. I am sad to say that I have too often taken the worst examples of what I am against, laid them alongside the best of what I am for, and "what do you know," my side wins—every time. I have lost count of the debates that do this. We scandalize the opposition while sanctifying ourselves. And when we do this, we never lose! But in reality, we never win either.

I will say more about this in the chapter on "Gathering at the Round Table." But for now, I want to propose that the way of love avoids this. Regardless of the issue, we take the best that one position has to offer and lay it alongside the best that other positions can provide. Only then can the conversation remain Christian.

Fifthly, the way of love is the way of accountability. On the level of secondary matters, I am accountable to do my homework and come up with the best reasoning and case that I can. Most of the time, this will mean that the first response is not to the person with whom I disagree but to myself; that is, to respond with the awareness that I must go and learn. For one thing, I have likely not framed my own views as well as I should. "Get it together before you take it on the road" is a good saying for us all.

But beyond this, I have almost certainly not done the hard work of familiarizing myself with views different from mine. So, becoming a student is step one in the accountability process. The way through controversy is not through superficiality, clichés, caricatures, and sound bites. It is through the time-consuming, energy-draining work of putting together the best thoughts that I possibly can.

In terms of the ultimate, I am accountable only to God. This does not mean, *I don't care what you think*; it simply means that *I cannot play to the crowd once I choose the way of love*. There is an "Audience of One," and I must think, feel, speak, and act in ways that I believe the One will approve. It is important to note this, because the way I am proposing in this book does not eliminate accountability. The most dangerous people in times of controversy are those who self-authorize themselves, without rooting themselves in the kind of accountability I am trying to describe.

Sixth, the way of love is the way of charitable discourse. This may be obvious from what I have said previously, but I want to be sure we are clear about this. And to be honest, there are numerous examples (especially comments on social media) where remarks are anything but charitable. If nothing else, I want to call out this inexcusable action, declare it to be unchristian, and forthrightly state that the way of love gives us no permission to communicate our views in ways that demean others.

Charitable discourse does not mean we all dress up, sit around fine-china dinner tables, and have polite conversation. It means that we enter into the conversation with basic respect in place. It means we choose our words carefully, using substantive language to communicate complex truth. If we are not willing to do this, we have not earned the right to speak—on social media, or anywhere else. I have growing worries that we are becoming unable to do anything other than throw word-grenades at each other in ultra-partisan ways. The way of love calls us to another approach.

Seventh, the way of love invites us into constructive cooperation. I will write about this at greater length, but for now it means that we ask ourselves and each other, "What is the highest aspiration we can aim for on this issue?" This is not impossible. There is always something. For example, in the debate about same-gender relationships, all sides might agree that not demonizing each other is an aim to which we can all aspire. If so, then that's what we go for. And we do not allow that aim to get lost as we move forward.

Finally, the way of love is the way of Christlikeness. I have saved this for last, because I believe the word *Christlikeness* is the highest word we can use to describe another person, place, or thing.

When Gandhi died, the Indian press (which was Hindu in perspective) described him as the most Christlike person the country had ever seen. And throughout the centuries, we have not found a better term to describe the highest and best.

So we must speak of the way of love in relation to Christlikeness. It is only in Christ that we will find the spirit, the substance, the strength, the stamina, and the skill to engage each other in ways that will enable us to move forward as God intends. But as with other things, a two-word phrase (*in Christ*) is largely useless, unless we can find some ways to describe what it looked like in Jesus, and what it might look like in us. I will devote the chapter entitled "A Way Forward" to this.

The way of love—the way we must use to restore the Bride to her intended beauty. This is the emerging vision that came to me during Lent in 2014. And that is all it is—an emerging vision, not a finished image. But like a sunrise, it can be put into words, even without knowing what the rest of the day will look like. The way of love is the way of God. If that were not so, none of us would be here, much less have the luxury of trying to find a way through the messes we create! Only because God's way is the way of love can we have breath to cry out, "Lord, have mercy! Christ, have mercy!" We must cry out this way—for the sake of the Bride.

Six

It's in The Book

When Paul wrote to Timothy that "every scripture is inspired by God" (2 Tim 3:16), he put into words the sentiment which Christians have held from the first century until now. I hold to that sentiment as I write this book. With John Wesley I can say that I am a "plain, old Bible Christian." But as with every Christian before me, I recognize that there are varying hermeneutical lenses through which we read the sacred text.

For Wesley and others back into early Christianity, it was called "the order of salvation."[1] It was, as I have said, a way rooted in the love of God and a theology of grace. The *ordo salutis* was a different hermeneutic than the ones used by Reformed and Lutheran theologians. It was similar but not identical to the interpretive principles held by Roman and Orthodox Christians. The point is simply this: When we say, "every scripture is inspired," we do not mean that we all interpret the Bible using the same presuppositions and principles.

The way of love is a biblical hermeneutic. It's in The Book. But when we adopt it, we then face the task of organizing the biblical message accordingly.

---

1. It is not my purpose to describe the various hermeneutical lenses that Christians have used, but we all have some means of organizing and interpreting scripture. There is no one-size-fits-all principle for doing this.

When we say that restoring the Bride of Christ to her intended beauty is a way of love, we then begin the task of interpreting the Bible in ways that produce the attitudes and actions to bring our aim to pass.

Theology starts with God: "theo-logoi" means "God words" or "words about God." And in the hermeneutical process, theology begins with revelation. Theology becomes our words about God only after we have received God's words to us. With respect to the way of love, we speak of God's nature as one of "holy love." To say God is holy is to speak of God's moral nature. To say God is love is to speak of God's disposition toward us.[2]

For most of us, this is exactly how our Christian life began. With a necessary recognition of God's holiness (rather than a self-righteousness we wrongly assumed), we were given John 3:16, which put the whole matter in the context of love—love for the world, which meant amazingly, "Love for *me*!" And from that beginning, we went on to unfold and declare, "You ask me how I know he lives; he lives within my heart." Amazing grace!

Given the primacy of revelation, and lying alongside it the necessity of our response, we entered into the world of spiritual formation: the never-ending process of becoming like Christ in thought, word, and deed. The way of love quickly became the way of life—abundant and everlasting. And as I write these words, and as you read them, we are both still caught up in the mystery and the magnificence of that life. Our little boats continue to float on the river of love. It is this reality, which not only causes us to interpret scripture as we do but also to engage in its application to all of life.

When my family and I visited countries in Europe, one of our plans included visiting the Louvre Museum in Paris. Room after room contained masterpieces, ancient and modern. In nearly every room artists had set up their easels, and were capturing the particular masterpiece in each artist's chosen medium. Some used pencil. Others sketched in charcoal. Some painted in watercolor; others in oil. Besides that, some artists were producing works that looked like photographs, while others were painting in more abstract styles.

What struck me was that all the artists were staring at the same masterpiece, but the magnificence of it, coupled with the gifts of each artist, enabled

---

2. There is no end to the books written on this theme. I would especially recommend Mildred Bangs Wynkoop's *A Theology of Love*, Randy Maddox's *Responsible Grace*, and Kenneth Collins's *The Theology of John Wesley: Holy Love and the Shape of Grace*.

a variety of paintings to emerge. I believe this is what hermeneutics does. It allows each interpreter to set up his or her easel, gaze at the masterpiece from a particular vantage point, and capture it in the medium and style that best communicates the artist's intentions.

I have chosen to set up my interpretive easel from the vantage point of love, and this immediately means that, while affirming the inspiration and authority of all scripture, I will be drawn into certain focal texts, using them to capture the angle I believe best serves the purposes of this book. If you have set up your hermeneutical easel elsewhere, all I can ask is that you respect my vantage point, even as I respect yours. As I see it, from my angle, the way of love beckons us to rise above our polarities and seek grace—for the sake of the Bride.

Seven

The Father's Love

There are multiple options for exploring the Bible on any given subject. I have chosen to use a trinitarian approach, looking to see what the Father, Son, and Holy Spirit have to teach us about the way of love. As I said in the previous chapter, the hermeneutic of love brings certain passages forward, not because they have more value than others but because they speak more directly to the purpose of this book.

In choosing this approach, I realize that I may leave out passages you feel are indispensable to any biblical interpretation of controversy in general or the same-sex relationships in particular. As you will see, I have not sidestepped the key passages, either in this trinitarian approach, or in some of the other chapters that will follow after it. If we are going to achieve a genuine third way, we carry the whole biblical message with us, not just the texts we use to leverage our position. But at the same time, I cannot speak of the way of love without asking you to ponder with me some passages that shed light on our goal to restore beauty to the Bride.

A trinitarian approach does not mean that I reserve certain sections of the Bible for a particular person of the Trinity. I realize that there is a trinitarian principle throughout the Bible. But for purposes of organization, I will focus my remarks about the Father to the First Testament, focus my chapter about the Son to the Gospels, and focus my chapter about the Spirit to the writings that complete the Second Testament.

In doing this, I accept responsibility for any limitations that emerge. You may choose to take what I present then reorganize it into another paradigm. But if you do so, I hope that I will have at least given you a portrait that contains enough color and form to be useful as you deal with the delicate and demanding issues that challenge the church today.

We begin our interpretation in creation. The impetus to make a world (or more likely, worlds) comes from a heart of love. God is not a narcissist. If that were true, God could have been content to remain in communion with God's own nature, for there is evidence (Gen 1:26) that there was some kind of inter-deity dialog going on. There is an "us" conversation going on during creation itself.

But this inter-deity dialog is not enough. God desired to relate to a creation, that is, to relate to everything that the world contains and represents. So if we are to begin our look at the way of love, we must begin with God's creation. And when we do so, we find that it is magnificent in both its macro and micro dimensions. Scientists continue to learn more about the cosmos by reaching as far into space as they can, and looking into the sub-atomic realities as clearly as they can. And the results are amazing.

Beyond our wildest imaginations, we are part of a creation that (at least to theologians) reveals the God of love. Every part functions with miraculous precision, and the parts fit together into a tapestry that is simultaneously mysterious and magnificent. And it is true to say, "God loves it all" (John 3:16). When we take this general assessment and focus it upon human beings, the created value of each person is beyond calculation, because each of us is made in the image of God. It is this assessment that provides the next step in our look at the Father—the act of redemption. Redemption only makes sense against the backdrop of prior value.

When our daughter, Katrina, was a little girl, she asked a question one evening after we read the story of Adam and Eve as part of our bedtime devotional. Listening to the story of the fall (even presented in language children could understand), Katrina was moved to ask, "If Adam and Eve messed up so badly, why didn't God just crumple up the world and make another one?"

This seemed perfectly natural to her, and not a bad thing, because it is what she would do when she spoiled a drawing she was working on.

I do not remember how we responded to Katrina that night, but I do know that her question stuck in my mind as the very question we should ask. And when we do, the only answer is found in the word *love*. God could not crumple up (destroy) the divine creation and start over. God's only option was to redeem the creation. That's what love does.

So that's what God did. In Genesis 3:8, we find God going in search of Adam and Eve. And when God found them, God clothed them in animal skins so that their nakedness and sense of shame did not have to remain exposed. This is what love does. And we see it in operation before three chapters in the Bible have passed by. Love redeems. Love will not allow anyone to be shamed.

Moreover, love never gives up. From the expulsion of Eden all the way through the rest of the First Testament, there is a cycle of success and failure, glory and embarrassment, righteousness and sinfulness, exile and return. The human story fluctuates, with wild swings between good and evil. Amazingly wonderful things are said and done, only to be followed by unbelievably horrible words and deeds. What does not fluctuate is God's love. It is the constant factor in the human roller-coaster ride.

But this kind of love is clearly not soft on sin. God always judges sin, but what God does not do is condemn the sinner. Instead, forgiveness is just a prayer away. Condemnation would be to crumple up the world (whether it be an individual or a community) and start over. Judgment is always exercised redemptively. That's what love does. In fact, judgment is only the first step in the restoration of love, where it has been lost by some thought, word, or deed.[1]

The next wave of the Father's love is revealed in God's conversation with Moses in Exodus 3:1–4:17. God says, "I've clearly seen my people oppressed.... and I've come down to rescue them." This conversation, and the exodus which comes from it, shows that God is never in favor of oppression,

---

1. Here is an early and significant insight from the Bible. God begins with judgment, but it is without judgmentalism. In other words, our kind of judgment is often directly opposite to God's kind. Judgmentalism leaves us condemned in our sin; redemption delivers us from our sin.

no matter what form it takes. Quite apart from the sinfulness that lies underneath it, any form of oppression is offensive to God, and we can be sure that God will be at work to deliver people from its evil.[2] We see this redemptive story repeated again and again in the exile/return pattern that continues to the end of the First Testament.

A further insight into the Father's love comes when God essentially fires the religious leaders and becomes the shepherd they have failed to be.[3] God will not allow sheep to starve while shepherds stuff themselves. God does not permit shepherds to default on their call to strengthen the weak, heal the sick, and bring back the lost. God opposes any shepherds who rule over their sheep with force and harshness. God despises the scattering of the sheep, which leads to the sheep beginning to feed on other sheep—following the example of their shepherds!

In describing the way of love, there is no greater tragedy than this. There is no depth to which a nation can fall than for its shepherds to be the very ones who fail to love. Taking this severe indictment to heart, we see why Saint Peter later said that when judgment comes, it *begins* within God's house (1 Pet 4:17).[4] I believe we are seeing this today, as the sinful ways of religious leaders are being exposed and a new generation of leaders emerges with a commitment to holiness of heart and life that some of us professionally religious types have forfeited. We are not yet through this purgative period, but whether we like it or not, false shepherds are only getting what they deserve! Lord, have mercy! Christ have mercy—on us all!

Finally, we can point to the Father's love through the emerging vision of a future, further, and final redemption, which leads somehow and someday to a new heaven and new earth. The vision begins in the First Testament,

---

2. It is impossible to deny that the issues pertaining to same-gender relationships create an oppressor group and an oppressed group. This dichotomy alone is sufficient to motivate us to do something about it; otherwise, we pray "deliver us from evil" in the Lord's Prayer in vain.

3. See Ezek 34 for a crystal-clear denouncement of the religious leaders—those who should have known better. Unfortunately, this theme continues into the Gospels, where we see Jesus's harshest words reserved for the legal experts, Pharisees, Sadducees, and other religious leaders who should also have known better. Those of us who are "professionally religious" should read passages like this with fear and trembling.

4. But as with any of God's judgment, even the judgment of the church is a "severe mercy," intended to bring us to our senses—to restore the beauty of the Bride.

as prophet after prophet looks toward the coming of Messiah, and beyond Christ's coming to the full restoration of God's kingdom.[5] How it all happens is complex, and different Christians view the culmination of God's will in various ways. But no matter what interpretation you give to it, "love wins." The Father's love is the supreme and prevailing love. We must seek this love, settling for nothing less.

This thumbnail sketch of the witness of the First Testament to the Father's love could be expanded into a whole book. The passages I have selected are sufficient to lay the foundation for a theology of love that comes to us through an exploration of the nature of God the Father. This initial examination intensifies as we move into the Second Testament, through the incarnation of Jesus and his giving us a vision of Abba. It is to this that we turn in the next chapter.

Before the biblical revelation has moved beyond three chapters, we stand in the presence of the Father's love—a love that will not let us go. A love that redeems and shepherds us, no matter what. After the flood in Genesis 7–9, God cannot and will not crumple up the world and start over. Redemption based upon love is the only option. Everything else either falls away by the weight of its own inadequacy, or is purged away by the restorative fire of God's judgment.

If we believe that we are to be like God, then the earliest creation story and the insights that follow in the First Testament make it clear that we are made and called to be a people of love. This book scratches the surface of what this means, but there is no doubt about the essence of our being or the nature of our mission—for the sake of the Bride.[6]

---

5. Unfortunately, some have mistakenly equated this kingdom with some version of a human kingdom. But the vision is greater and grander than that. I recommend E. Stanley Jones's *The Unchanging Person and the Unshakable Kingdom* to see the vision described in scripture.

6. This book is only a primer on an exceedingly greater story. It is like trying to describe a baseball game by looking through a knothole in the outfield fence. Even our best efforts are incomplete. We see enough to get the essence of the game.

Eight

The Son's Photograph

J esus said, "Whoever has seen me has seen the Father" (John 14:9). This
sentence creates a seamless tapestry of revelation between the Father and
the Son, causing some to say that Jesus is the best photograph of God
ever made. Without a doubt, Jesus puts a face on God, and the face is one of
love. As with the chapter on God the Father, there is no way to chronicle that
revelation comprehensively. But the following passages weave their way into
the hermeneutic of love that forms the interpretive principle for this book.

We must begin with the incarnation itself. The Word became flesh (John
1:14), and this enfleshment was both to express and to illustrate the nature of
God toward the world. One of the first verses (John 3:16) we are taught when
we become Christian—"God gave his only son"—is sometimes offered to us
as a grand vision for our lives even before we become Christian. It is amazing
how this single sentence can be accepted but then not used to help shape a
way of love in the midst of controversy.[1]

Among all the ways that Jesus personified the life of love was his befriending of people who were unwilling to be friends with each other. This
revelation was one of the major revisions that I made during Lent of 2014. I

---

1. I am convinced that on the matter of love, the Bible is crystal clear. Yes, there are some
other passages that are difficult to understand and to interpret, but not when it comes to the
mandate to love God and others. Equally clear is God's displeasure when we do not do this.

could not overlook the fact that Jesus created a circle of friends that included religious leaders and those whom they condemned. This insight became one of the pillars in my belief that Jesus' life and ministry was the incarnation of a third way and a motivation for my seeking one today.

Jesus's willingness to make friends with the Pharisees and the ordinary people tarnished his reputation in both camps. The Pharisees were offended that he fellowshipped with sinners. And surely the crowd must have wondered (at least initially) what his motives were in befriending them. I can easily imagine a kind of arm's length relationship from those on the left and those on the right. But then it dawned on me that Jesus was not operating on the basis of his reputation; he was operating on the basis of love, the same kind of love the Father had been demonstrating for billions of years—love for every created person, place, and thing.

The second observation about Jesus flowed from this initial one; namely, that Jesus said he had not come to destroy the Law, but to fulfill it. He said this because he knew that law-oriented people conclude someone is breaking the Law when they see that person operating with something other than a dualistic, right/wrong mindset, or coming down on what they perceive to be the wrong side of the Law. In fact, Jesus knew some of the religious leaders would never believe he was fulfilling the Law. But that is what God's Son said, and we should take his claim seriously.

When we do, we discover that he moved the Law from a performance-orientation to an intention-orientation, an orientation that operated on the basis of the two commandments. A performance orientation allows us to base our spirituality on *what* we do, but an intention-orientation moves us to base it on *why* we do it. The message is rooted in the motivation.

In a strictly law-oriented system, we do what we do because we *have* to.[2] But in an intention-oriented system, we do what we do because we *want* to. And our willingness is fueled by the internal motivation of love, not an external system of expectation. Ironically, the intention-orientation gets the job done, but it does so for an entirely different reason and with a different spirit.

---

2. The culture of Jesus's day was an honor/shame one. This kind of environment is ripe for the rise of a performance-oriented religion, because when we do it right we are honored as good, but when we do it wrong, we are shamed as bad. Jesus's intention-orientation takes both our attitudes and our actions out of the honor/shame system and puts them into the environment of love.

The intention-orientation does not ignore the Law; it fulfills it—and that is exactly what Jesus said he had come to do.

So, for example, Jesus says that adultery is not essentially a sexual act outside of marriage; it is a lusting spirit that can wander even within marriage—not a behavior so much as a mindset. And so it is with other aspects of the Law. We live from the heart, and the things that are in our hearts will eventually reach our mouths, eyes, ears, hands, and feet.[3] Love dies from the inside out. That is why Jesus told us to guard our hearts. When we do, we fulfill the Law.[4]

The third observation about the Son is found in what is arguably his clearest exhortation: "Do not judge" (Matt 7:1). I have read a variety of interpretations about this, most of which try to find some escape clause underneath what seems to me to be a crystal-clear instruction. The word in Greek for judge is *krinō*.[5] In addition to communicating a condemnatory attitude, it also includes the idea of doing so from an alleged superiority—a superiority that often includes hypocrisy; that is, a judgment of someone or something when we ourselves are either committing the same sin, or another one.[6]

Jesus showed his affinity with this view when he asked why people glare at the speck in someone else's eye, but completely ignore the log in their own (Matt 7:3). There is just no getting around it—we are *not* to live this way, period. There is no person, place, or thing that gives us permission to violate this principle. By giving us this command, Jesus is essentially saying, "Judging is not your job; it is God's job. God is the only one who can judge another person correctly. Your job is to pay mind to your own life and to your relationship with God."[7]

---

3. This is why we must keep watch over our lives, paying close attention to the outward manifestations of emotion that can quickly change reasoned discourse into unchristian vitriolic. When this happens, we must ask ourselves, "Where is this coming from? And why?" Often, we will find it is not emerging from anything close to righteous indignation—which is what we usually like to name our outbursts.

4. In the next chapter about the Spirit, we will see the connection between the Law and the fruit of the Spirit (Gal 5:22-23).

5. This brief overview of *krinō* comes from William D. Mounce's book, *A Complete Expository Dictionary of Old and New Testament Words* (Grand Rapids: Zondervan, 2006), 371.

6. This point will be revived and intensified when we look at what Paul has to say about the whole matter in the chapter "Paul Weighs In."

7. In the chapter entitled, "The Witness of Tradition," we will see how this principle was put into practice.

A fourth insight comes from what I call Jesus's "top shelf" approach. By dealing compassionately with the woman caught in the act of adultery, and by touching the persons with a skin disease, Jesus was using one of the big-ten sins, and ultimate cultural shaming, to illustrate the way God feels about people across the board. This is the principle of defining the principle by expressing it at the highest level. If Jesus was willing to forgive an adulterous woman (who was supposed to be stoned), and willing to put his hands on a person infected by disease (who was supposed to be shunned), this is the Bible's way of telling us that God places no one outside the reach of divine love.

But with all such examples of the Son's love, we have not yet reached the pinnacle. There is no greater expression of love than the cross. Steven Manskar observes, "Atonement is central to the gospel of Jesus Christ because God is love. Love is a relationship characterized by giving the self to and for another person."[8] Jesus had already said that there is no greater love than when people lay down their lives for their friends (John 15:13).

And then he did it! By using the word *friends* to describe those for whom he died, he found in the cross yet another way to say and demonstrate the love of the Father for all people. As his followers, we walk the way of the Cross, which calls us to the same kind of self-sacrificing love. It remains the most radical way of living ever seen on the earth.

E. Stanley Jones put the same idea into these words, "Jesus on the cross is God, not smashing His enemies but melting them. There is only one way to get rid of your enemies, and that is turn them into your friends, and the only way possible to turn them into friends is to love them."[9] I read these words during Lent of 2014, and they put one more platform plank into my conviction that the way of love is the only way forward.

And so the Son's love is a reflection of the Father's love. When we recall that the Son is the Bridegroom, we can only imagine how much the Risen Christ wants his Bride to be gowned (adorned) with the same kind of love, and how grieved he must be when he sees her siblings tearing her gown to shreds, leaving only self-righteousness visible, and too much nakedness exposed. We must seek anew the life of Christlikeness—for the sake of the Bride.

---

8. Steven Manskar, "Wesleyan Leadership Blog," April 8, 2014.

9. E. Stanley Jones, *Growing Spiritually*, 124.

Nine

The Spirit's Witness and Work

Referring to the Holy Spirit, Jesus said, "he will take what is mine and proclaim it to you" (John 16:14). Through this statement, Jesus completed the link that established the symbiotic relation-- ship between and among the persons of the Trinity. He had already linked himself to the Father, and now he linked himself to the Spirit.[1]

Because of this connection between the Son and the Spirit, the essence of Christlikeness has been defined as the fruit of the Spirit: love, joy, peace, patience, kindness, goodness, faithfulness, gentleness, and self-control (Gal 5:22-23). Christians down through the centuries have maintained that we cannot claim to be in Christ if we live in opposition to these qualities. The essence of holiness and the virtuous life is defined by these nine words.[2] We can take these nine words and use them to evaluate our attitudes and actions in relation to others. We are never allowed to violate the fruit of the Spirit.

---

1. In John's Gospel, Jesus speaks of his relationship to the Father by referring to himself as the "sent one" by the Father, and by his dependence upon the Father, to the extent that he said he did not say or do anything unless he was told to do so by the Father. His ultimate declara- tion was, "I and the Father are one" (John 10:30).

2. E. Stanley Jones spends nearly 100 pages to describes Christlikeness in terms of the fruit of the Spirit in his book *Growing Spirituality*.

The fruit of the Spirit is the essence of what Jesus was speaking about in John 15, when he told his disciples to remain in him, declaring that when we do, we will bear much fruit (15:5). Jesus is speaking of the same fruit that Paul describes. In my own tradition, John Wesley found John 15 to be so central that he chose it as the text to be read at the annual Covenant Renewal service. When he came to write his explanatory notes on Galatians 5:22-24, he noted that these nine qualities are lived by "they who belong to Christ."[3]

Moreover, the fruit of the Spirit is the evidence that we are led by the Spirit. Paul's exhortation for us to be so led in Galatians 5:18 leads into the kind of life that emerges as we are filled with the Spirit and walk in the Spirit. And as you may already know, love is the first dimension of the fruit of the Spirit.[4] We would expect Paul to write this, given that he calls love "the better way" in 1 Corinthians 12:31. Love is the genesis of the Christlike life. And the nourishment which fruit gives is not reserved for only certain kinds of people.

One of the powerful aspects of the fruit of the Spirit is that they transform us inwardly and outwardly. That is why they have often been used to describe holiness of heart (inward holiness) and life (outward holiness). They are the ways we fulfill the two great commandments. When we look at each of the nine words, we realize how each is both an attitude and an action.

We cannot *do* loving acts unless we *are* loving people. We cannot be patient unless we are patient. And so on. Each manifestation of the fruit in an act is made possible because we have first tasted of the fruit of our own lives and become what each dimension of the fruit is. The fruit of the Spirit is the connecter of the being/doing life. We cannot separate the inward and outward dimensions of the fruit of the Spirit and claim to be Christian.

As with the other chapters about the Father and the Son, I have only taken note of a few illustrative passages with respect to the life of love as revealed in and through the Holy Spirit. But the Spirit's involvement in the formation of the life of love is verified by Jesus himself when he said, "You

---

3. John Wesley, *Explanatory Notes Upon the New Testament* (Naperville, IL: Alec R. Allenson, n.d.), 697.

4. Some scholars believe that love is *the* fruit (given the verb in Gal 5:22 is singular), with the other eight words expressing a particular manifestation of love. Others view the fruit as being a unified description of the Spirit-filled life. Either way, love is where it all begins.

will know them by their fruit" (Matt 7:16). We cannot find a more encouraging word than this, but it comes wrapped in great challenge.[5]

As I look at the current controversies in the church, what grieves me most is that I see Christians failing to relate to each other on the basis of the fruit of the Spirit. Our disagreements are too often devoid of the fruit of the Spirit. And it is not surprising then that we turn to relate to others without the fruit of the Spirit defining our attitudes and actions. The fallen world sees mean-spirited Christians. They do not understand this, and they shouldn't!

The desire of the Holy Spirit to produce the life of love in us, and our failure to allow the Spirit to do so, has created the basis for the world's rejection of Christianity. The sadness is that they have made their rejection based on waxed fruit, not the fruit of the Spirit.[6] And so we come to the end of this chapter saying once again, "Lord, have mercy! Christ, have mercy!" We come needing to be filled by the Spirit anew—for the sake of the Bride.

---

5. The encouragement is simply that we do not manufacture the fruit of the Spirit. It is the outcome of being filled with, led by, and walking in the Spirit. Or to say it another way, the Spirit-filled life is a life made possible by grace. The challenge is to take this reality and manifest it everywhere, every day, to everyone.

6. Somehow, God is going to have to make this right. Some people will die, having not rejected true Christianity, but the pseudo versions we have put before them. I am confident that the just and loving God will have a way prepared for everyone to have the opportunity to see the real thing. The grief comes when we realize that we Christians did not bear witness to true faith as we should.

Ten

Paul Weighs In

The way of love is rooted in and reflected by the Father, Son, and Holy Spirit. This is as it should be. All theology begins in the Godhead in one way or another. But thankfully, the Bible combines divine revelation and human response, creating a holy conversation, which some have called a sacred dance. We turn now to the human dimensions of the way of love, finding in scripture itself a powerful confirmation to what we have seen thus far. The confirmation comes through none other than the Apostle Paul.

When I read E. Stanley Jones's statement citing Paul as one who said, "I am controlled by the love of Christ," I was stopped in my tracks.[1] I was not stopped because it was the first time I had ever considered the way of love through the writings of Paul; I was stopped because I had not previously realized that Paul openly and forcefully declared love to be the orienting principle of his life. The Greek word for "controlled" describes a person who is led by love—one who pursues the way of love on every occasion—one who runs swiftly after love and seeks it eagerly.

In Lent 2014, this recognition was transformative for me. In a new and fresh way I saw how Paul developed his theology of love, beginning with

---

1. This is the way James Moffat translated 2 Cor 5:14. Moffatt's translation was one of E. Stanley Jones's favorite translations.

the affirmation that it is "the better way" (1 Cor 12:41), followed by the marvelous description of love in 1 Corinthians 13, and then climaxed by the exhortation to "pursue love" (1 Cor 14:1). In the span of slightly over one chapter, Paul had moved from an affirmation of the way of love to a personal embrace of it—an embrace that he then extended to the rest of the Christian community.

When we make love our *pursuit*, it is the motive for every moment of our life. It is the controlling principle (to refer back to Stanley Jones's statement) for every situation. We use love to direct our thoughts, words, and deeds—allowing nothing to pass muster that violates the way of love. Far from being a sentimental ethic, it is actually the hardest thing in the world to do; impossible apart from a deep work of grace in us. The way of love challenges every expression of egotism (the fallen and false self) and calls us into a life of holiness, where love fills our hearts, expelling everything else that is in opposition to it.[2]

Paul's affirmation is the most radical ethic ever offered to the human race. It is an ethic that removes all clauses and caveats, giving us no wiggle room to say that another way of life is "okay in this case." Paul's affirmation eliminates the option of claiming that some cause justifies uncharitable words and actions toward any person. In Lent 2014, I was gripped by a vision of what the world might look like if we truly and fully adopted the way of love.

All of this came rolling into my life through the witness and writing of Paul, the very person most-often cited as having the harshest words with respect to same-sex behaviors. Whereas before I had managed to keep his interpretive words separate from his writings about love, I could no longer do so. And when the two came together, I found myself having to wrestle with a Paul I had never seen before. Setting up my easel before the masterpiece gave me a new vantage point for restoring the Bride to her intended beauty.

With this new perspective, I went to Paul's words about same-sex acts, beginning with the extended passage in his letter to the Romans (1:18–2:5).[3]

---

2. I will say more about this in the chapter entitled "A Clue in My Own Tradition."

3. In studying this passage it was important for me to remember that there are no chapter and verse designations in Paul's letter. These were added much later. As you will see, this has become significant in my interpretation, and it has enabled me to see that even in this strong writing, Paul is still controlled by love.

Much of the teaching I had been exposed to, and almost all of the derogatory comments I had been seeing in social media focused on 1:26-27, where Paul speaks of same-sex acts as "dishonorable." And without coming down on one side or the other in this controversy, I have to say that the passage itself is quite clear; Paul is not in favor of these kinds of acts. And his additional references to same-sex acts in 1 Corinthians 6:9 and 1 Timothy 1:9 continue his negative interpretation.

So how are we to take these hard words of Paul and keep them in the context of the way of love? That was my challenge, and I believe it is the challenge of all Christians. Without the way of love, we are left with no option but to use Paul's words as hammers, or to try to find some way to diminish or dismiss what he is saying. But if we keep the way of love in place, I don't think we have to settle for one option against the other. My challenge now is to try to find the words to tell you why I have come to this third-way consideration. It rests upon two foundational pillars.

First, when I read the passage in its entirety, I saw that in addition to shameful sexual acts, Paul lists *twenty-one* additional acts that are to him as negative as sexual acts between persons of the same gender.[4] So, when we come to the end of chapter one, we have twenty-two items on the list of sins, not just one! And to make the point even more clearly, Paul lists things like covetousness, envy, deceit, gossip, haughtiness, and boastfulness—so at the end of the chapter we realize that every single one of us is on Paul's list! Every one of us—no exceptions! No one can read Paul's list and still be standing at the end. We are left on our knees, confessing that "all have sinned and fall short of God's glory" (Rom 3:23)—declaring that "there is no righteous person, not even one" (Rom 3:10).

When I read Paul's words this way, the Holy Spirit spoke to my heart, asking, "Are you getting this? Really *getting* it?" I had to confess that I had failed to get it so often in the past, but was awakening to something absolutely transforming when reading Paul's words through the way of love. The transformation was in relation to the earth-shaking truth of the universality of sin—something that is almost always missing when one side in a controversy

---

4. In the chapter "Questions That Remain," I will turn specifically to the sinfulness of inappropriate sexual acts. For now, I am making a larger point about the way-of-love paradigm.

43

condemns or mocks the other side. I saw that this is the damaging result when dualistic thinking prevails.

By its nature, dualistic thinking (left unchecked) demands that there be a hierarchy, a position from which one group can look down upon another group. And since no side can stand the thought of being the inferior one, what we end up with is every group claiming to be the higher one, the true one. What we end up with, in addition to the issue being debated, is the clash of egos, with each side determined to win. Thinking ourselves to be prophetic, we are actually obnoxious toward those who disagree with us.

The absolutely radical nature of Paul's word is this: there is no hierarchy. No hierarchy! None whatsoever! Based on the Psalms, Paul connected with the Judeo-Christian tradition that says:

The Lord looks down from heaven on humans,
to see if anyone is wise,
to see if anyone seeks God,
but all of them have turned bad.
Everyone is corrupt.
No one does good,
not even one person. (Ps 14:2-3)

Before we establish a confessing movement, the way of love calls us to have a confessional moment—a movement that aligns with God's perspective, described this way in Psalm 143:2, "no living thing is righteous before you."

And this realization led me into the second discovery I made while reading Paul's words—the discovery that non-judgment is the way Christians are to follow.[5] As I write these words, I am still pondering what this meant for Paul, and what it must mean for us today. I cannot capture the impact of these words with only one section of one chapter to describe them. It is here where I realize how much praying and working I have yet to do. Dualistic thinking has been my way too long, leading me to think that I *must* judge—that not to

---

5. In the chapter "The Witness of Tradition," I will show how fully the early Christians carried out this principle. It was only later in church history when we modified the principle in various ways—sometimes abandoning it altogether.

do so would be unchristian. I am only in the early stages of believing that this is not true, but even with miles to go, I have to do my best to tell you why I am viewing judgment from a different vantage point.

For one thing, I am viewing it from the very passage we are examining. As soon as Paul creates his twenty-two-item list, he immediately says, "So every single one of you who judge others is without any excuse. You condemn yourself when you judge another person because the one who is judging is doing the same things (Rom 2:1)." The universality of sin demolishes the option of serving as the judge and jury. Demolishes it! And the amazing thing is that this is exactly what Paul writes—what he must write if he is, indeed, controlled by love.

Notice the words he uses. He applies the principle of non-judgment to everyone: "every single one of you." He gives us no wiggle room, making it clear that we are "without any excuse" because we "are doing the same things." If we are going to call Paul's words in this passage harsh, then we must also see that they are as harsh on judgment as they are on naming the twenty-two things to start with. To see either dimension without the other is to miss or misinterpret Paul's message.

The picture became even clearer for me when I remembered that the Greek word Paul uses for *judge* in this passage is the same one Jesus used in his crystal-clear prohibition against one person judging another one (Matt 7:1)—a word used to describe a judgment that takes place from the vantage point of alleged superiority and does so with a condemnatory tone. Jesus and Paul are one in saying, "Don't do this!" And again, the Holy Spirit came and asked me, "Are you getting this? Really *getting* it?"

At this point in my Pauline journey I was not ready for what happened to me next. I saw as incorrect the often-alleged charge that people are unbiblical if they take something other than a hard-line view. I came to see "unbiblical" as a word used to cut off conversation and to stigmatize other views that are different from our own. I saw how conservatives and liberals have *both* leveled this charge at each other. I saw that, at least for me, the real issue was that I had not been biblical enough! I had read these words without considering the full impact of what Paul was saying, both to those of us who live in these ways but also to the Christian community who must respond in some way to them.

45

I saw how Paul is calling us (both as actors and assessors) to a radical humility, and then I realized that in the Christian tradition (and particularly in the Wesleyan tradition of which I am a part), humility is considered "the mark of love." Humility is the leveling agent, the eliminator of *all* hierarchies. It is the factor that makes us confessional on the one hand, and nonjudgmental on the other. No exceptions.

I came to see that any attempt to excuse myself from Paul's list is false and hypocritical. And I came to see how doing so leads to a counterfeit stance for dealing with my own sins, and the sins of others. It is not the way of love, because it lacks humility. Simply put, judgment is not my job. Another influential writer, Billy Graham, has said the same thing: "It is my job to love, the Holy Spirit's job to convict, and God's job to judge."[6]

Perhaps you have entered into this view more quickly and easily than I have. I hope so. But if you have been as I have been, I can only implore you to read this over and over until you are gripped by the radical nature of Paul's words. We are without excuse, either as to the universality of sin, or to an alleged attempt to be judges concerning it. To both excuses, Paul says a clear, "No!"

And then, in addition to Paul's affirmation of the way of love and his interpretation of sin and judgment, I saw it all working out in his ministry: the ministry of reconciliation. In Ephesians 2:14, Paul wrote that God has broken down the dividing wall of hostility between Jews and Gentiles—that is, between Jews and the rest of humanity. If this is truth, I have no permission to build up a new wall of hostility between myself and anyone else. No permission. To do so is to undo the work of Christ.

Furthermore, with the wall removed, we are given the ministry of reconciliation (2 Cor 5:18-19), a ministry that is a sign that we are "in Christ" and that "the old things have gone away" (2 Cor 5:17). Given what we have already seen about sin and judgment, this is not suddenly becoming soft on sin (which is the false charge leveled at those who take something other than a hard-line view); rather, it is being committed to a ministry that seeks to unite fellow sinners in a new way of living together—a way of turning enemies into

6. A statement attributed to her father by Gigi Graham-Wilson in a sermon delivered to a seminary chapel on April 10, 2014.

friends. How could anyone possibly see that as an easy task? No, Paul is asking us (as did Jesus) to do the hardest thing in the world—to love, no matter what, no exceptions.

All this culminates in Colossians 3:1-17, with Paul writing in verse fourteen, "And over all these things, put on love." I have come to see this passage as the high-water mark in Paul with regard to the way of love. Through Paul, of all people, I have become even more firmly convinced that the Bible is instructing us how to live with respect to controversy in general and the same-gender marriage issue in particular. We're just not listening and obeying as we should.

"The love of Christ controls us," Paul said. And his affirmations, his writings, and his ministry show that he was controlled by love! Eugene Peterson paraphrased 2 Corinthians 5:14 in *THE MESSAGE* to include, "This puts everyone in the same boat." Indeed it does! And it means if we continue to poke holes in the boat, we all sink. It means that when we refuse to stop shredding the Bride's gown, we expose our nakedness too. Paul has weighed in to tell us so—for the sake of the Bride.[7]

---

7. For the sake of time and space, I will not write about the witness of John and Peter to the way of love. But it is visible there too, particularly in 1 John and in 1 Peter, both of whom look to Jesus as the example of the Christian life—the one who lived the way of love and calls us to do the same. They tell us to put away all malice and to live the life of love.

Eleven

The Witness of Tradition

When we step outside the Bible and enter into the world of Christian tradition, the interpretive task continues to be nothing short of impossible.[1] But despite the limitations of any hermeneutic, and apart from the limitations of space in this book, it is nevertheless possible to chart the progress of the way of love in Christian history. Sometimes we see what happens when the way of love is abandoned or ignored. At other times, we see the beauty of the Bride when it is affirmed and activated. By contrast and comparison—by abdication and affirmation—the way of love still shines through.

The witness begins with the first Christians who lived after the Second Testament era. In the early 100s, a document called *The Didache* was written.[2] It is thought to have been an early catechism that Christians used to preserve

---

1. I want to keep before you my own sense that by attempting to describe the way of love, I am (at best) only establishing one vantage point—one that does not address every question that can be asked of it or rise above every charge that can be leveled against it. But even with that recognition I still maintain that the way of love is "the better way." Yet it is a way (as we shall see) that cannot be fully developed apart from the input of the larger community. No single person or group holds the patent on it.

2. References to *The Didache* are from the 1894 translation by Charles H. Hood, published variously, including a Kindle eBook version in 2012. *The Didache* is published in chapters and verses, so references look like biblical ones.

and pass on the faith, as it became clearer that Christ's return would not occur as soon as many had previously believed. As the original apostles died, the need to do this was essential.

The Didache opens with six chapters about "the two ways." And what we see immediately is that the way of God is the way of love. The early Christian community is exhorted to love and pray for enemies, following the teaching of Jesus and those who came after him in the Second Testament. The way of love is the basis for belief and practice—for message and morality (1:3).

One aspect of this is the teaching for Christians to do everything possible to avoid schism: "Thou shalt not desire schism, but shalt set at peace them that contend" (4:3).[3] Remarkably, one of the means for doing this is the refusal to convict anyone of transgression (4:3).[4] As the Christian church developed over time, this instruction went more and more into eclipse, with periods of church history showing that Christians not only became judgmental but actually thought that judging is God's will. We have some very sad epochs in our history when that was the case. For now, I only want to show that it was not so in the earliest days of the faith.

This does not mean that these early Christians overlooked sin. It only shows that they had a different way of dealing with it than we often have today. In terms of human sexuality, there are numerous references in *The Didache* to sexual immorality, adultery, and infidelity.[5] This is an extra-biblical confirmation that the Christian sexual ethic was, from the beginning, a contrast to the often-prevailing mores of the cultures where Christianity spread. But it is also an illustration of how the way of love was the undergirding principle for dealing with sexual immorality.

As Christianity continued into the second and third centuries, we find present the same commitment to the way of love. Benedicta Ward's edition of

---

3. When I read these words, I realized that this is precisely the purpose for this book. Everything I am writing is intended to produce what *The Didache* called for nearly two thousand years ago—a purpose consistent with the overall witness of Christian tradition.

4. I will say more about this principle in the next section of this chapter, when we look at the practice of non-judgment in the early Christian community. The key word in this particular instruction is *convict.*

5. In the chapter entitled "Questions at the Table," I will write specifically about these things, for I have come to see them as crucial in our interpretation of same-gender relationships.

the *Verba Seniorum* provides challenging and compelling illustrations to this effect.[6] The sayings begin with the theme "progress in perfection," which is essentially an exhortation to live the two great commandments—the essence of the way of love. The first monks lived personally and communally in relation to the virtuous life, which is marked by love.

With this foundation laid, the collection goes on to describe additional dimensions of the Christian life. The way of love creates subsequent attitudes and actions that Christians are to embrace. For our purposes, and in keeping with what we have found in Jesus and Paul, one of the themes is the practice of non-judgment. Amazingly, these early monks refused to pass *judgment* (as previously described in the Greek word which describes it) on another person, even when there was no doubt that the other had sinned. The collection contains a dozen sayings and stories to show the extent to which this practice was maintained. For this book, I will reference only three of them.

> A brother sinned and the presbyter ordered him to go out of church. But Bessarion got up and went out with him saying, "I, too, am a sinner."

> A brother asked Poemen, "What am I to do, for I become weak just by sitting in my cell?" He said, "Despise no one, condemn no one, revile no one: and God will give you quietness, and you will sit in peace in your cell.

> A hermit said, "Do not judge an adulterer if you are chaste or you will break the law of God just as much as he does. For he who said "Do not commit adultery" also said "Do not judge."

As clear as these stories are, the other nine are even more revealing, because they are longer and go into more detail about the ways and means the monks used to avoid passing judgment on others. As with some previous portions of this book, I do not know how long you will need for the radical nature of these teachings to sink in. But I can only encourage you to take whatever amount of time you need for them to do so. During Lent

---

6. Benedicta Ward, *The Desert Fathers: Sayings of the Early Christian Monks* (London: Penguin Books, 2003). The *Verba Seniorum is* the systematic Latin collection of early-monastic stories and sayings, compiled around 550 CE. It contains eighteen themes, one of which is non-judgment.

of 2014, they made their way afresh into my mind, descending into my heart.

The absolutely astounding thing is that these early Christians did not pass judgment even when there was no doubt that the person had sinned. They refused to do so precisely on the basis of love, which (as we have seen previously) includes the recognition that all have sinned, and that there is no righteous person—not even one! As they lived this conviction, the monastic community said, "This is the true way of salvation."[7] Standing on the foundation of that irrevocable conviction, they had to find other ways to deal with sin in their midst. Essentially, it was what Billy Graham commended in the remark I attributed to him in the previous chapter—that it is our job to love, the Spirit's job to convict, and God's job to judge.[8] These early Christians followed the exhortation of Saint Macarius of Egypt, that Christians must "embrace in their hearts all people of the world, without distinction between good and evil."[9]

To limit the exploration of the way of love in the Christian tradition to the first five centuries is insufficient, but necessary in a book like this. All I can show is that a trajectory was laid in the Bible and in the Christian community that emerged in the next four hundred years. After that, we see it repeated in the lives of such people as Benedict of Nursia, Bernard of Clairvaux, Francis, Clare, and Julian of Norwich, to name a few. For myself, as a Christian in the Wesleyan tradition, I have found it expressed in the life and ministry of John Wesley. I turn to his witness in the next chapter.[10]

I close with the following summary of the witness of the overall Christian tradition to the way of love. I see it manifested over and over again in the following principles and practices:

---

7. Ward, *The Desert Fathers*, 86.

8. In the chapter entitled "Questions at the Table" I will gather up the witness of scripture and tradition to propose how this classical principle might be applied today.

9. Macarius's homilies, in *Patralogia Graeca*, Vol. 34, p. 639.

10. To be transparent and fair, spread across the centuries are numerous teachings against same-sex practices, teachings given by some of the most prominent church leaders in Christian history. I will deal with this undeniable fact in the chapter entitled "Questions at the Table." For now, I am continuing my effort to show that the foundation for what has come to be called "living faith" is the way of love. Without this, we cannot interpret the teachings and practices of Christianity. Everything rests on the living out of the two great commandments. We go off the rails if we forget this.

1. protecting every person from harm, whether they be victimized by words or deeds, individuals or groups, by the church or the government;

2. elevating not one sin above another but keeping the reality of universal sinfulness paramount, along with the need to maintain the spirit of humble confession;

3. refusing to use convictions as weapons against another human being, even those who have undoubtedly sinned; and

4. standing against efforts to divide the church along lines of ideology, working instead to do everything possible to preserve unity in the Body of Christ.[11]

My Lenten journey of 2014 immersed me in reading and pondering these kinds of things from a wide array of witnesses in the tradition. I became personally convicted for all the ways I have intentionally and unintentionally (knowingly and unknowingly—by commission and omission) violated the classical way of love. I can only change my heart and life, hoping never to do so again—for the sake of the Bride.

---

11. This fourth principle is the delicate but necessary distinction between doctrine and opinion. Through the creeds and confessions of historic Christianity we have our basic beliefs. The rest is what theologians have come to call *opinions*, and these should never become a rationale for schism. In the Wesleyan tradition, we are heirs of this particular distinction.

Twelve

A Clue in My Own Tradition

For a long time I have known that John Wesley's beliefs, life, and ministry could be summarized as a "theology of love." I have understood Methodism to be rooted in the principles and emerging practices of the two great commandments, essentially understood in the phrase, "holiness of heart and life." I have seen that his theological system is an order of salvation (*ordo salutis*),[1] with God's grace being the foundational dimension. I have noted how the structures of early Methodism were intentionally connected to this order, so that what God willed could become reality in the lives of people.[2]

But it was during Lent in 2014 that all of this, and more, became focused on the issue of divisiveness in general, and in particular to how it is playing out in the issue of same-gender relationships. As never before, I was convicted to take my knowledge, experience, and participation in the Wesleyan tradition, and apply it to the current issues that threaten to divide us, and to the

---

1. By choosing this hermeneutic, John Wesley was consciously identifying with the early Christian paradigm that I have just discussed: "the way of salvation," essentially interpreted as a way of love in relation to the two great commandments, the fruit of the Spirit, and the practice of non-judgment.

2. I have written in detail about this in my book *The Way to Heaven: The Gospel According to John Wesley* (Grand Rapids: Zondervan, 2003), which is a revised edition of *John Wesley's Message for Today,* published in 1983.

formative and deformative ways we are dealing with them. Here is what has emerged from that contemplation.

I began my exploration on the top shelf—Wesley's belief in Christian perfection.[3] He stepped onto the path of the holy-living tradition and made it the orienting principle and guiding passion for Methodism. He believed that Christ had come into the world to save us from sin, so that we could then be free to live a life that expressed the love of God and neighbor. He called this "love filling the heart," and it is this perspective that gives us our overall picture of the Wesleyan tradition.

He drew from scripture and primitive Christianity for this perspective.[4] Some of his significant sources in the tradition were the desert fathers—saints such as Macarius of Egypt, John Chrysostom, Basil, Gregory of Nyssa, and Gregory of Naziansus. In these leaders he found the basis for a theology of love. We can use John Cassian as an illustration that reflects a host of other people whom he used for guidance.

The Conferences of John Cassian provided a glimpse into early-Christian theology in the second and third centuries, especially the life of self-denial and the life of love that emerges when we are abandoned to God. St. Benedict used Cassian's work as he prepared his rule of life that has influenced untold numbers of monks and Christians at large.[5]

In the very first Conference, Cassian says that he sought out Abbot Moses for guidance in the life of Christian perfection. In a conversation covering twenty-three chapters, Abbot Moses gave Cassian an extended teaching, rooting Christian perfection in the two great commandments and using the

---

3. If this theology is new to you, let me simply say that you must not read a dictionary definition of perfection into Wesley's theology. Wesley is using the word in what he called its "scriptural sense." It is not flawlessness, but fullness. It is not perfect performance, but purity (singleness) of intention. It is orienting all your life in relation to the two great commandments. In previous chapters I have referred to this perspective, calling it a way of love.

4. "Primitive Christianity" is a phrase that describes the period from approximately 100 CE to about 500 CE. Wesley was among those who believed that this period was superintended by the Spirit in ways that enabled it to be a point of reference for future Christians. He saw this particularly in the development of the creeds, and also in the principle of universal truth; that is, what has been believed by the majority of Christians, in the majority of places, the majority of the time.

5. Edgar Gibson, trans., *The Conferences of John Cassian* (New York, 1894). I am using the *Christian Classics Ethereal Library* e-book edition as the source for my comments.

way of self-denial (humility) as the means for living the life of love which the commandments envision.

Everything is rooted in one's aim. That is, everything begins in what you desire. The life of love begins in the heart before it can be manifested in the life. By using the analogy of the archer, Abbot Moses showed how before the arrow flies, the archer lines up toward the desired target to hit. In terms of the life of love, it is the target we want to hit, and our aim is the hermeneutic we use to line up toward it.

Nearly 1700 years later, Wesley and the early Methodists seized upon this paradigm, making it the defining element of their faith and practice. They often called it "holiness of heart and life," which was nothing other than the expression of the two great commandments in everyday living. Holiness of heart was the synonym for the first commandment (love of God) and holiness of life was the synonym for the second commandment (love of neighbor). These were never to be separated, any more than you can separate inhaling and exhaling in breathing.

With this foundation in place, the means of grace (spiritual disciplines) became the instruments for actualizing the life of love in the believer—with the Instituted Means of Grace providing the way to holiness of heart and the Prudential Means of Grace providing the way to holiness of life.[6]

Moreover, the ministry structures of the early-Methodist movement were designed to create the life of love in relation to inward and outward holiness. The Societies were the place for people to awaken to grace. The Classes were the place where they could attach to it. And the Bands were the place where they could advance in the grace and knowledge of the Lord Jesus Christ.

Even in Wesley's early days at Oxford University in the Holy Club, we can see the influence of the life of love upon him and those who met daily to seek after God. The club members regularly evaluated themselves in relation to twenty-two questions. All of them are insightful, but two are of particular interest to our examination of the Christian life in relation to divisive issues.

---

6. The Instituted Means of Grace (also called works of piety) are prayer, searching the scriptures, the Lord's supper, fasting, and Christian conferencing. The Prudential Means of Grace (also called works of mercy) are doing no harm, doing all the good you can, and attending the ordinances (public expressions) of God.

Question 19: Do I thank God that I am not as other people, especially as the Pharisee who despised the publican?

Question 20: Is there anyone whom I fear, dislike, disown, criticize, hold a resentment toward, or disregard? If so, what am I doing about it?

These two questions (to say nothing of the others) embody the very principles I have previously described in the chapters dealing with Jesus and Paul: the principle of humility and the accompanying practice of non-judgment. As Methodism became a movement after 1743, these same sentiments were incorporated in the *General Rules of the United Societies*, the questions for the Class meetings and Band societies, and also for John Wesley's own daily questions for self-examination. As Wesley wrote, the way of love was "the prevailing influence" for a Christian's attitudes and actions.[7]

Before leaving this consideration, we can use two of Wesley's standard sermons to further illustrate his commitment to the way of love. The sermon on "Christian Perfection" is a powerful exposition on the life that is rooted in the two commandments and the deliverance from sin that it provides. And his sermon on "The First Fruits of the Spirit" adds to the larger picture the priority of the fruit of the Spirit in the life of the believer. To "walk after the Spirit" is purely and simply walking in relation to the two commandments and in relation to the fruit of the Spirit at work in our lives.[8]

What we see in the Wesleyan tradition is a remarkable movement of God that "spread scriptural holiness" (the life of love) across the land, and eventually around the world. The paradigm of love does not eliminate or minimize the reality or negativity of sin. But for Wesley, as for others before and after him, the way of love is the context into which we put all other aspects of the Christian life. We are never free to abandon love in order to establish any other principle.

John Wesley knew that his approach would not be heralded by everyone,

---

7. John Wesley, *Explanatory Notes Upon the New Testament*, 656—a note in reference to 2 Cor 5:14, which we have referred to previously.

8. The sermon, "Christian Perfection," can be found in *The Works of John Wesley*, Volume 2 (Nashville: Abingdon Press, 1985), pp. 97-124, and the sermon, "The First Fruits of the Spirit," can be found in *The Works of John Wesley*, Volume 1 (Nashville: Abingdon Press, 1984), pp. 233-247. Both volumes are edited by Albert C. Outler.

and he experienced rejection and opposition throughout his lifetime, with some of the most-severe persecution coming from fellow Christians in the Church of England. When confronted with this, he responded, "If we cannot all think alike, can we at least not all love alike?" And as a further recognition that Christians would come to differing conclusions about things, he wrote in the sermon on "Christian Perfection" words that we all need to take to heart as we face our differences:

> Hence, even the children of God are not agreed as to the interpretation of many places in holy writ: Nor is their difference of opinion any proof that they are not children of God on either side.[9]

And so, my revisiting of my own tradition during Lent 2014 provided me with a fresh reminder that I have chosen a vantage point of faith that is rooted in the way of love as given to me through scripture and tradition. My longstanding commitment to holiness of heart and life has only increased during this recent revisiting of the Wesleyan perspective. In fact, I see the life of love in a more radical way than ever before. All I can hope to do is to be faithful to this perspective as I live my own life, and to be proactive in commending it to others—for the sake of the Bride.

---

9. *The Works of John Wesley*, Volume 2, previously cited. From the sermon, "Christian Perfection," p. 102. (Wesley's paragraph 5 in his first major point.)

Thirteen

Intermission

When we attend dramatic presentations, there is almost always an intermission. It not only provides us a time to get up, stretch, and walk around—it also gives us a time to process the play as we have seen it thus far. It helps us to gather the various sub-plots and characterizations into the meta narrative that will resume when the intermission is over. Intermissions are not just time-outs, they are important for a good understanding of the drama itself.

I believe that now is a good time for an intermission so far as the development of this book is concerned. I have spent a fair amount of time developing the way of love as the paradigm given to us from scripture and tradition—the paradigm which I believe we too often abandon when we face divisive issues. We never completely leave the language of love, or the insistence that we are doing "the loving thing" with respect to the words and deeds we use to assess others. But just ask the folks who are on the receiving end of our attitudes and actions, and they will be quick to tell us that the ways we relate to them do not feel like we are loving them.

We can either take their responses seriously, or we can march on in whatever cause we have used to justify our words and deeds. What I am trying to say thus far is that the Bible and the Christian tradition call us to a profound reconsideration of what the loving thing really is. What I am trying to say thus far is that we can move away from the way of love without even realizing it.

The point is simply, once we realize we have done so, what are we going to do next? And the purpose of this book is to say, "We must return to the way of love, and do so with a radical commitment to it." Such was my experience in Lent 2014, and I have tried to communicate that in a variety of ways in the previous chapters. More especially, this book is a call to find a third way that enables the sides of the debate to bring their best to bear upon finding a new way to move forward in the future.[1]

I have called this third way the way of love, because I can see no better way for regathering and moving forward together, even through the most challenging of times. I am convinced that a fresh and more-radical application of the way of love is (as it has always been) "the better way." The rest of the book will be an attempt to turn theory into practice—what a growing number of Christians today are calling "lived theology"—what John Wesley himself referred to in his time as "faith working *by love*."[2] But before we turn to that, I want to create an intermission that we can use to summarize where we have come so far, preparing ourselves for the practical applications of the way of love. Briefly recalled, I see the following key points in the way of love.

First, it is the way of the two great commandments. If Jesus said that everything is summarized here, we can look for no better unifying principle for ourselves. What we must do, however, is ponder the transformative dimensions of these commandments as they exist to produce holiness of heart and life in us.

Second, the way of love is the way of grace. This means that we move forward in the spirit of humility—the classical evidence of the way of love. Grace accepts us as we are, but it does not leave us as we are. But for grace to work in our lives, we must start with the confession that "all have sinned"—that "there is none righteous, no not one." Without this, dualistic thinking skews the debate by causing each side to posture itself as superior to the other. The way of love levels the playing field, bringing us together as nothing other than

1. This too is a gift provided to me through the Wesleyan tradition, a tradition whose theology as an order of salvation has been called a third way.

2. Italics mine.

sinners saved by grace. And as has always been the case, our confession of sin leads to unforeseen and miraculous deliverance and cleansing—what Jesus referred to as abundant or full life (John 10:10).

Third, the way of love is the way of the fruit of the Spirit. Once emptied of pride and presumption (the fallen world's false self), we can be filled with the Spirit. And when we are, these nine dimensions empower and direct inward and outward holiness: love, joy, peace, patience, kindness, goodness, faithfulness, gentleness, and self-control. Paul said that there is nothing against the Law in any of these expressions; that is, we are never going against the will of God when we live in these ways. This is the way of Christlikeness. And so the fruit of the Spirit becomes the "North Star" for navigating our way through times of difference and controversy. No exceptions.

Fourth, the way of love eventuates in the practice of non-judgment. Again, no exceptions. To judge is to fall back into dualistic thinking, which creates the false perception that one person can somehow be judge-and-jury over another person. As we will see in the next section of the book, this does not mean we are soft on sin, but it does mean that we deal with it in other ways.

To practice non-judgment means that we are gripped and held by the realization that it is our job to love, the Spirit's job to convict, and God's job to judge. As often as necessary, and as long as it takes, we bring ourselves back to this conviction. And we do this even when other people have clearly sinned in thought, word, and deed. There is no more radical application of the way of love than this.

Fifth, the way of love aims at nothing short of reconciliation. The history of Christianity has patterned us toward schism. But the way of love is the way of union. It is living against the backdrop of Jesus' prayer in John 17—that we may all be one. And by the very nature of the word *reconciliation*, our efforts are made in the presence of enmity and opposition. That's what reconciliation is—coming together *despite* our differences and staying together (in prayer and conferencing) until the fresh wind of the Spirit blows a new way forward into our lives.

My experience during Lent 2014 taught me that the way of love is much harder than I had previously thought it to be. I agree with Richard Rohr that "being over against is a lot easier than being in love."[3] In fact, as I write these words, I have come to see that the way of love is one that I have not fully embraced or practiced in my life. Everything you are reading in this book is in relation to my own failures to live the very life I am now commending. I have simply come to the place where I can no longer accept this. I confess my sin.

In this intermission, I can only invite you to get up, stretch, and walk around. You may want to do this literally. But at least I hope you will experience a "pause that refreshes" and ponder what I have tried to say so far in the book. I invite you to do this, knowing that some of you will have already taken offence at the ways I have tried to describe the way of love. Your vantage point may simply not have prepared you to consider this one. Or you may be somewhat like me, realizing that even an espoused commitment to the way of love can fall short of the actual living of it. And even if you are devoted to this way and practicing it ahead of where many of the rest of us are, this intermission can be a time to renew your commitment and to seek additional ways to apply the principle in the future.

Whatever your situation may be, I ask you to lay this book down and enter into a time of prayer. Ask the Holy Spirit to put you within the way of love as never before. I am convinced that this is happening more and more in the Christian community.[4] I join with those who believe that a "new Pentecost"—a "new reformation"—a "new great awakening"—a "great emergence" (or whatever you may call it) is already underway. And it goes without saying that I cannot imagine this taking place in any other way than the way of love—and all for the sake of the Bride.[5]

---

3. Richard Rohr, *Everything Belongs*, revised and updated edition (New York, Crossroad Publishing Company, 2003), 22.

4. I have written about this in my previous book, *Fresh Wind Blowing* (Salem, OR: Wipf and Stock, 2013).

5. When I use the phrase "for the sake of the Bride" I am not ignoring the world that desperately needs the way of love as well. I am only restating my conviction that renewal begins in the Body of Christ, as the Bride is restored to her intended beauty. From there it will spread and grow. The witness of love can only come from a church rooted in love.

Fourteen

Gathering at the Round Table

W hen E. Stanley Jones arrived in India in 1907, he found almost every expression of the Christ-and-culture relationship.[1] He found, for example, Christianity so identified with British colonialism that Indian religions and culture were often in opposition to it. Moreover, he found stereotypes and caricatures of Christianity being used to dismiss the relevancy of Christian faith. And even worse, he found Christians themselves divided along a variety of ideological lines—including competing views of what evangelization should look like.

Consequently, Jones concluded early on that the way forward could not be through a presentation, or even a re-presentation, of Christianity. It was an amazing and controversial conclusion, but one he felt compelled to embrace. Instead, he chose to move through the person and work of Jesus and the way of Christlikeness.[2]

His Christo-centric approach can be seen in all of his books, with the culminating affirmation that "Jesus is Lord." Jones wrote that when he made

---

1. H. Richard Niebuhr, *Christ and Culture*. This book remains a classic, but one that is being revisited and critiqued by some today. I use it to show the classical paradigm, and one that would have been more in vogue in Stanley Jones's day—even though Niebuhr had not written his book when Jones arrived in India.

2. E. Stanley Jones, *Christ at the Round Table* (New York: Abingdon Press, 1928).

Jesus the center, the circumference (that included such things as other religions, cultural challenges, etc.) found their proper place. And, he found that Christlikeness could be found in varying ways and degrees in every religion. Christlikeness became the magnet that attracted people of Christian faith, other faiths, and even people of no faith.

But affirmations alone were not enough. Jones also realized that there had to be a practical manifestation of conviction. There had to be some concrete way to bring people together who had previously been at odds with each other. He sought for that way in prayer, and he found it in what he called the Round Table.

Similarly, I have become convinced that the way forward with respect to divisiveness in general and same-gender relationships in particular cannot be found through Christianity. There are too many camps and sides—and they are engaged in a multi-decade debate that shows no signs of stopping. Christianity has splintered into so many parts that it is nothing short of impossible to come together on the basis of theological position. The varying positions are themselves expressions of dualistic thinking, as one viewpoint is deemed superior to another. This sets in motion a never-ending disagreement, with each party citing righteousness for itself and declaring (either directly or by inference) unrighteousness for the opposing view or views.

My entire tenure as a United Methodist clergyperson has been in this environment, and as a businessman told me some time ago, "If we kept trying to find a solution to our problems the way Christians do, we would have gone out of business a long time ago." I agreed with him then, and after more years of controversy, I believe it even more now. In fact, I am willing to propose that we have already gone out of business so far as the highest and best of Christianity is concerned. At least, that is what I experienced as I pondered all these things during Lent 2014. Whether or not we even dare to use the language of love in our current dilemmas, we have walked away from a full-fledged practice of it—both with respect to the way we relate to each other as Christians, and in the ways we treat those outside the church with whom we disagree.

And so, as we come to the second section of this book, I want to envision a new round table. I believe it is the practical basis for the way forward. But it has been out of use for so long that most of us need a refresher course in what it was when E. Stanley Jones first used it.[3] Instead, we have our tables, but nearly all the time only those who are on our side are invited to sit there. Even when we have multiple tables, we set up a head table to be sure the dominant view prevails. Psychologically, we have to wonder where the fear-factor plays into this decision. Sociologically, we can see our usual practices as expressions of ethno-centrism. But whatever the case, the round table has not been the dominant way of addressing controversy in the church in my lifetime. Instead, we have created "war tables," where we assess the strength of our enemy and devise tactics to defeat them.

But the way of love calls for another approach, and I believe Stanley Jones found it in the round table. Indian religion and culture found it amazing more than a hundred years ago, and it remains an amazing option for us today. In this chapter we will explore the key elements of the round-table process.

The process begins by recognizing the place of the round table. Theologically, it is the place where faith, hope, and love come together. We come with faith, believing that we honor God by gathering in the name of Jesus. We come with hope, believing that if we stay together the Spirit will break through in some way to enable us to move to a place that is better than current reality. And we come with love, the kind of love we have been describing in the previous chapters of this book. The round-table process is a concrete expression of the ancient Christian trilogy of cardinal virtues.

This means that the round table is the place of respect. We come believing that God is at work in all people of faith and good will. But we also come confessing that it is possible to concentrate on our position so much and for so long that we either lose sight of other positions—or—caricature them in order to make our position look stronger or better. A return to the spirit of respect does away with that false notion, and enables us to say, "God is trying to speak to us, and God will use all of us to construct that message."

---

3. E. Stanley Jones would agree that he did not invent the round table, but rather rediscovered the historic Conciliar effort, which Christians have used over the centuries. Through this classical practice, Christians have been able to produce Creeds, Confessions, and to resolve significant issues. John Wesley used the Annual Conference to similar ends in Methodism. Happily, there have been some expressions of the round-table principle in my lifetime, and they have helped shape my conviction regarding its usefulness today. One of them is called "Appreciative Inquiry."

This respect is connected to reality—a reality in which there is no avoidance of any issues and questions that have to be dealt with in order to make progress.[4] All parties are invited to bring their questions—to leave nothing behind—to declare nothing off-limits, but rather to engage everything in the spirit of respect that we have just noted.

The round-table process connects respect and reality to the aim of reconciliation—a theme we have previously examined in this book. The process rejects any caricature that "light cannot fellowship with darkness," and in its place puts the conviction that everyone at the table has some light. The round-table process is a serious version of the song we have sung since we were children: "This little light of mine; I'm gonna let it shine—let it shine—let it shine—let it shine!" As spiritual scientists, we come to the round table believing that the various colors of light can converge into Light, and that we can realize again that "God is light, and there is no darkness in him at all" (1 John 1:5).

When I went back to the writings of E. Stanley Jones about the round table, I left convicted that we have too often failed to manifest the spirit that the round-table approach fosters. To gather in the name of Jesus with respect, reality, and reconciliation controlling our attitudes and actions would be a departure from the way too many of the tables are set up today.

But the process is only launched by the spirit of the table. It continues in the steps that are taken when the group gathers to engage in holy conferencing. E. Stanley Jones goes into detail about these steps, but for the sake of this book (which is only an introduction to this and many other ideas), I will only write about four essential practices.

First, the round-table process gathers the best people that each viewpoint has to offer. We have only to look at today's comments on social media to realize there is a broad spectrum of wisdom, emotion, and conviction expressed in relation to every divisive issue. Some are, quite clearly, unchristian even though they still claim to be. Others are muddled, and still others are not much more than warmed-over versions of ideas that have kept us stuck for too long.

---

4. In the next chapter I will write about the kinds of questions that must be brought to the table with respect to same-gender relationships. There is no way to be other than selective, even in illustrating the process with respect to one issue. All other issues have their unavoidable questions as well.

But on every issue there are credible and respected persons who can come to the table and present a particular view with the right spirit and substance. E. Stanley Jones looked for these in India, and as he found them, he invited them to the round table. We must call the best representatives into the round-table experience.[5] We must ask them to use their preferred means to prepare the best case they can for the view they hold.

Second, at the round table, we compare the best with the best. Too often we set up an artificial situation where we take our best and compare it with someone else's worst.[6] Whenever we do this—guess what?—we "win." But it is a victory based on incomplete information and jaundiced views. The victory we claim is actually no victory at all. Instead, at the round-table, we discuss differences in relation to the highest and best versions we can articulate. Anything else is unfair.

Third, every representative is allowed to speak without interruption. Listeners may take notes that they will return to later, but at this stage one person speaks, and everyone else listens. This practice is not only an expression of the principle of respect; it is also the cultivation of attentiveness—a quality that is necessary if progress is to eventually be made. Interruptions always sidetrack the round-table process, and sometimes the discussion ends up in places where the presenter never intended to go, losing the main point in the spate of comments that are attached to it. We see this often on social media.[7] Instead of this, the round table moves forward with each person being permitted to speak without interruption.

Fourth, when the case is on the table, questions of clarification are then allowed. Notice that at this point they are questions of *clarification*, not debate. Listeners are allowed to ask for an expansion of an idea. They are free to ask for more information about something. But they are not allowed to debate the presentation by inserting their views into it. The clarification process

5. Assuming for now that the best we can do is to set up the round-table experience within judicatory groups, I can only commend each denomination or parachurch organization to follow this practice within their own ranks.

6. One example of this in the sexuality debate is when the conservative side fails to include male-female pedophilia, but highlights same-sex acts of it. From the outset the debate is slanted—headed in the wrong direction.

7. "Talk Show" radio and television programs are another example of it.

continues until both the presenter and the listeners are satisfied that the best possible case has been made.

These four key practices continue in a recurring cycle until the group believes they have put on the table the best possible case (made up of the varying parts) for the issue at hand. This fact alone should be enough to show that the round-table process is not one that happens quickly. In fact, the round-table process denies any notion of a quick fix. The issue that has divided the community for too long has taken a protracted period of time to unfold and become as divisive as it has. It will not be resolved quickly. So the round-table process assumes that the participants are committed to being together for a longer time than is typical of a three-day conference or short-term symposium. Only those who are committed to holy conversation over an extended period of time should be invited to the round-table experience, for it will inevitably move in a little-by-little fashion, under the direction of the Holy Spirit.

It goes without saying that this entire process is bathed in prayer. Participants are prayerfully chosen. The spirit of the table is maintained by intermittent prayer, including confessions by the group when the good spirit is being eroded in some way. As the group moves from one presentation to another, they pray with gratitude for the opportunity to hear a substantive case, and they ask God to reveal where the light is that everyone needs to see and carry forward.

All of this culminates in the potential of the round-table experience. Simply put, it is the experience of being peacemakers, of the kind Jesus commended in the Beatitudes (Matt 5:9).[8] The round-table process is an ancient-future expression that Jesus Christ began through his theology of God's kingdom—a kingdom where people from every tongue, tribe, and nation would gather to worship and serve God. Even before the end of the Second Testament, this was being lived out as the Gentiles were included along with Jews in the third-way community called the Christian church.

In our day, we have the witness of Pope Francis in this approach. Within the first year of his leadership, he set in motion conciliar efforts that have the

---

8. I believe this is why E. Stanley Jones included in his writings *The Christ of the Mount*. He saw this as Jesus's inauguration speech, launching God's kingdom (the ultimate paradigm) in ways he went on to practice and expected his disciples to practice as well.

potential for peace making in the Roman Church, but beyond it as well. We can only pray that his vision and efforts will result in outcomes toward which the way of love points. In his first Apostolic Exhortation, he set the pattern for the kind of dialog needed for us to move forward,

> In this way [the way of peace-making] it becomes possible to build communion amid disagreement, but this can only be achieved by those great persons who are willing to go beyond the surface of the conflict and to see others in their deepest dignity. That requires acknowledging a principle indispensable to the building of friendship in society: namely, that unity is greater than conflict. Solidarity, in its deepest and most challenging sense, thus becomes a way of making history in a life setting where conflicts, tensions, and oppositions can achieve a life-giving unity. This is not to opt for a kind of syncretism, or for the absorption of one into the other, but rather for a resolution that takes place on a higher plane and preserves what is valid and useful on both sides.[9]

What Pope Francis, E. Stanley Jones, and others like them all point to is the fact that the way of love must be made concrete through determined and sustained efforts. Without this, Christianity will have failed; it will not have been tried.

Restoring the round table has always been one of the most controversial acts ever undertaken. E. Stanley Jones, for example, lost friends within and beyond Christianity as he activated the round-table concept in India. Pope Francis is already received criticism from Roman Catholics for his early conciliar efforts. Looking back farther into church history, we see that those men and women who decided to enact the way of love through concrete means were often declared "unbiblical" by one group or another. But they knew that the way of love was "the more excellent way," and they persevered despite opposition. We are called to do no less in our day—for the sake of the Bride.

---

9. Pope Francis, *The Joy of the Gospel* (Washington, DC: USCCB, 2013). He officially gave this teaching to the church and to the world on November 24, 2013.

Fifteen

Questions at the Table

Earlier in this book I told you that I would not sidestep the challenging issues and difficult questions related to same-sex love. This is the chapter where I intend to keep my promise. I have waited until now, not to postpone the inevitable but rather to do my best to model an approach to the difficulties that I believe offers hope for the future. I believe we too often jump into conversation and debate without committing ourselves to a prior spirit (the way of love) and to a necessary process (the round table). We go at it with no holds barred—something neither the paradigm of love nor the process of holy conversation allows. So I have gone to lengths deliberately to lay the groundwork—even in the way this book is written—for addressing the obvious and formidable questions that cannot be avoided.

But in doing so, I ask for your help and participation. I know already that this will be the lightning-rod chapter for many readers. Based upon decades of observation and participation with respect to same-sex and gender issues, I know that my presentation will attract some and repel others. But at the round table, the issue is not agreement or disagreement. It is the determination to seek the guidance of God into a higher way for all.

So I ask you not only to use your mind as you read this chapter, but also to use your imagination. Imagine that you have been invited to the round table. You are prepared to make your presentation when your turn comes.

73

But now it is my turn. And as one committed to the round-table principles described in the last chapter, you are committed to respect what I am about to write, and to give your attention to it—without judgment or criticism. Yes, that is a tall order, but it is the only way you can read this chapter in the context and with the spirit that must attend it.

If all this chapter does is to further shred the Bride's gown, it should not have been in the book at all. But if it can serve as an example of how a way of love can proceed at a round table, then (by God's grace and favor) I pray it might serve a useful secondary purpose within the larger purpose for which I have written this book. There can be no way forward if we lack the courage to address the key questions that always come up. I believe that to omit this chapter would be to make this book artificial or hypothetical.

So I ask for your participation on the basis of what this book is seeking to accomplish—to make a call for a third way forward in the ways that we deal with controversial issues in general and with the same-gender relationships in particular. But to do that, as Pope Francis reminded us in the last chapter, is not to seek syncretism "but rather for a resolution that takes place on a higher plane." Whatever else this means, it means that we look squarely into the face of the tough questions, bring our best prayer and thought to them, and believe that the Holy Spirit can work in our midst for good.

Because this book is only an introduction to a much larger and detailed experience, I cannot presume to deal with every question that I have heard or asked regarding same-sex identity and practice. But I do intend to look at the following selected questions, which have prevailed for nearly fifty years in The United Methodist Church and even longer in the larger Christian tradition. I will be candid enough to let you know where I currently stand in relation to them, but also generous enough to frame my responses to leave room for you to bring your best case to the table as well.[1] So, here are some of the key questions we face with respect to same-gender relationships, and my best thought for each.

The first question that almost always arises early on is this: *Are homo-*

---

1. Admittedly, using a book format to do this is not a pure expression of what would occur at the round table, for the group format is conversational, not printed. But what I am writing in this chapter is an illustration of what I believe desperately needs to take place, even if the context and format is different.

sexual practices a sin? "Sides" are ready to pounce on this with their varying viewpoints, but rather than that, we need to put the question on the table and engage it without jumping to any conclusion. When we do, we find that every reference to same-sex acts in the Bible is put in a negative context. This is where some stop, draw their conclusions, and leave the table. But the question is not closed at that point, and the conclusion is not as cut-and-dried as it might first seem. To make the same-sex issue a one-question conversation is to fall back into dualistic thinking.

Instead, we must go on to ask, "What kind of sexual act is the Bible against?" And while there is no consensus on that question, a growing number of scholars are looking at the Hebrew and Greek words used to describe same-sex practice, and rightly noting that they are *behavioral* words, not orientation or identity words.[2] To the extent that this is true, it means the Bible's declaration of sin pertains to inappropriate *acts*. Being homosexual, knowing innately there is sexual attraction to the same gender, is no more sinful than being heterosexual, knowing innately there is sexual attraction to the other gender. But all Christians (whether attracted to the same or other sex) are held to standards of holiness that preclude *acting* out their orientation in ways that are declared sinful by scripture.

The sixteenth-century word for these sinful acts is *fornication*. In contemporary English the word is translated as "sexual immorality." It is the word used in the Bible to describe any sexual act that is practiced outside the bond of marriage. With respect to single persons, pre-marital sex is fornication (a form of sexual immorality). With respect to married persons it is adultery (a form of sexual immorality). With respect to every person it is also any act that sexually harasses or abuses another person. It is any act that turns a human being into an object of gratification, whether directly or indirectly through the media, through sex trafficking, or through the pornography industry. All such acts are what the Bible declares to be sinful.

When viewed this way, *all* Christian men and women should be able to

---

2. This is a very complex issue—as are all the ones we will consider in this chapter. My comments are only meant to provide some overview to things that demand more extensive study. I urge you to go beyond anything here (as I myself am doing) to encounter deeper dimensions of key points. I can only hope that what I write will provide some windows for determining where this additional study is called for.

unite in efforts to oppose any attitudes or actions that demean another human being. This would include the recognition that a person's sexual orientation (in and of itself) is not sinful, but how that person expresses his or her orientation may be so.

By taking this position outside of the Bible, we see the ongoing opposition to gay and lesbian identity. There is too much to consider in the succeeding twenty centuries since the close of the Second Testament, so I am going to limit my comments to the period from 100 to 400 CE. Even here there is too much, but a look at the major views shows a pattern emerging.

Beginning with *The Didache* and continuing up to the *Apostolic Constitutions*, there is an unwavering condemnation of same-sex acts. The main concern is the sexual abuse of young boys by older men (pederasty), but the concern is not limited to this single sin. It continues with general prohibitions against fornication (sexual immorality) and adultery, whether of same-sex or male-female expression.

As I read through the writings of the first four hundred years, I cannot ignore this universal concern. I have chosen this period because it is approximately the same period that I used to establish the practice of non-judgment in early Christianity. So the question becomes: "How do we reconcile what seems to be extreme mercy on the one hand and extreme concern on the other?" This is a question that must be brought to the round table.

I suggest that the reconciliation lies in two dimensions. First, the concerns in Christian tradition (as in the Bible) are aimed at sexual *acts*, not orientation. For example, Basil the Great exhorts monks not to yield to the temptation to abuse boys. The thing to note is that he is exhorting *monks*—men who were already Christian and had taken the holy vows of poverty, chastity, and obedience. The line is drawn, not at the monks' sexual orientation but at the improper enacting of their orientation.

The second dimension lies in the persons themselves. They have professed faith in Christ and in some cases made solemn pledges leading to holy orders. Having done so, they are accountable to the community to be faithful. When they are not, individuals in the community practice non-judgment, but the community itself holds the members accountable to commitments they have publicly made.

76

So with respect to the first question, it appears that the focus of concern is not upon a person's orientation but on how they live out that orientation. More work obviously needs to be done in scripture and tradition to bring this possibility into greater light, but it is not untenable to hold it. It seems to be the overall approach by the first Christians—a way of love that includes both the acceptance of orientation, yet holding persons accountable regarding how they act out that orientation—and this for male-female couples as much as for same-sex couples.

A second key question is this: *Can two people of the same gender fall in love the same way that a male and a female can fall in love?* [3] Some would say that even going this far is too far, but on what basis can we draw a line that limits how one person can feel love and relate to another? In the Bible we see deep relationships formed by persons of the same sex, and while none of them can be definitively labeled as sexually intimate, they do reflect how love between persons of the same sex can exist.

It is possible for two women to say, "I love you" to each other, and it is possible for two men to say the same to each other. Love is a quality of life that is not reserved for persons of a particular sexual orientation. Moreover, to say this to a person of one's same sex does not mean that either person will act out the implications of that statement inappropriately. I do not know of any writer in my time who has emphasized the way of love more than Henri Nouwen. But we know he was gay. Yet he lived out his orientation with celibacy and with fidelity to the pledges he made as a priest. Nevertheless, Henri said genuinely to all sorts of people, "I love you," and it was not only the expression of his heart, but he believed also an expression of God's heart.

This leads quickly to a third question: *Can there be such a thing as same-gender marriage?* Ironically, this question is difficult to answer in part because the culture is running ahead of the church in trying to frame a response to the question and to supply the ethos for it. This should not surprise us, for

---

3. You may notice that I am not exploring these questions beyond the gender differentiation. I realize that the issues expand into bisexuality and transgendered matters. These further complexities are outside the scope of this book, and way beyond my ability to speak to them. My generation has grown up and lived through the controversy primarily with the homosexual-heterosexual distinction. I must leave it to other Christians to articulate the more nuanced responses that attend the LGBT environment. However, I do believe that my responses can be used in discussing these additional topics.

we do not live in an age where the church is consulted first. Sometimes it is not consulted at all. The church is no longer the nation's conscience. But this fact leaves us having to play a version of "catch up" when it comes to the issue of same-gender marriage. Even as I write these words, more and more states are grappling with the question and making marriage between people of the same sex a civil-rights issue.

For theology, the question turns on how we define the word *marriage*. If it is viewed only as a male-female union, then clearly, same-gender couples cannot marry. But if we go back to the first question in this chapter, and use the Christian opposition to fornication or sexual immorality as a focal point, then the question expands into other considerations. Paul does the same thing in 1 Corinthians 7:9: "It's better to marry than to burn with passion." Like the first Christians, we must wrestle with the definition of marriage at the round table.[4]

And that is exactly what Christian same-gender couples are trying to tell Christian male-female couples.[5] They are trying to say, in every way they can, that they do *not* want to "live in sin" any more than men and women would. And the option for avoiding sexual immorality is the same for same-gender couples as for male-female couples—establishing a lifelong union based upon promises, monogamy, and fidelity. Consequently, if we define marriage in terms of the morality of it, rather than the gendered dimension of it, we find that there could indeed be same-gender marriage.[6] In this sense it is possible

---

4. Let me be clear: I do not think that the only, or even the primary reason for marriage is to avoid sexual immorality. We do not *define* marriage that way. There are many other metaphors that make marriage the beautiful, exciting, and wonderful thing that it is. But with respect to human sexuality, this is one dimension that must be factored into the round-table conversation.

5. Here is a place to remember that this book is only written for Christians who are engaged in trying to figure all this out. The civil society does not view morality or marriage the way Christianity does. I am simply trying to lay parameters for holy conversation among those persons who have made a prior profession of Christian faith. Social apologetics would have to proceed along different lines, but not without reference to the Christian view.

6. The question of same-gender marriage appears to be the most hotly debated question in both the society and the church. If "marriage" is more about the nature of the union than about the gender of those being united, we have a legitimate basis to speak of "same-sex marriage." But it is not a double standard. In fact, the Christian standard (no sexual immorality, adultery, or infidelity) is higher for either straight or gay people than the fallen-world cultures make it.

for two people of the same gender to pledge themselves to the exact same commitments that men and women do—and then to be held accountable by the same standards within the Christian community.

A fourth question is raised by church history: *Has the Christian church ever condoned same-gender marriage?* For a long time, I would have said, "No, absolutely not." But in the spirit of the round-table process, I have come to realize that an absolute denial of this possibility is more the result of what we have been taught than what might have possibly been the case. So as a further example of not sidestepping key questions, I must deal with this one.

Within scripture, we can say that the only kind of marriage portrayed in it is marriage between and man and a woman. This began in creation with Adam and Eve, and it continued to the end of the Second Testament era. Key passages can be noted as the Bible unfolded, including Jesus's comments about marriage as a man leaving his father and mother and cleaving to his wife.

So the question we are dealing with is not specifically addressed in the Bible. But within the Bible we do find passages that surface the previous question about the morality of marriage. Paul, for example, is concerned with how marriage is being violated in the Corinthian church. There is no reduction in opposition to sexual immorality and adultery in the Bible. There is no doubt that the values of sacredness (solemn pledges), monogamy, and fidelity are foundational to any understanding of Christian marriage.

Any response to the question of Christianity condoning same-gender marriage must be sought outside scripture. At best, the Bible is silent on the matter, but the most credible biblical scholarship has never used an argument from silence as the foundation for a particular position. It may be helpful in some ways to take note of what the Bible does and does not address, but there is no warrant for using biblical silence as consent or prohibition. In somewhat the same way that the United States Supreme Court interprets the Constitution regarding matters that it does not specifically address, we are left in the Christian community to interpret the current question outside specific biblical information. We must turn to the Christian tradition for help.

When we do so, we find that the evidence across the centuries is largely supportive of male-female marriage. There can be no debate on that fact. But this realization does not close the door regarding whether or not same-gender marriages have ever been performed in the Christian community. We have to do some extra homework in order to determine that.

When we do, we discover limited evidence that there may have been some same-gender marriages performed by the church. The major advocate of this position was John Boswell, professor of history at Yale University.[7] Almost from the day Boswell published his findings and offered his convictions, people who both deny and support LGBT rights have criticized his scholarship.[8]

This leaves us with a very confused conversation about this question. I almost skipped it for that reason, but clearly a lot turns on whether or not the Christian church has ever performed a same-gender marriage. Boswell uses about sixty texts from across the Christian world—and texts that span centuries—to assert that there was such a thing (until about the eighteenth century) as Christian marriage for gay and lesbian people. Critics either deny this, or re-interpret the liturgies (which do exist) as pertaining to something called "brother making" or "sister making."

Again, the issue is complicated and clouded. But no matter what we call these services, they were performed. For me, an equally significant question is why they ceased to be performed. All of this is beyond my ability to evaluate, and beyond my purpose for this book. But it is a question that must be considered at the round table. As with the issue of how the Christian tradition interpreted same-sex acts as sinful, so too how the Christian tradition viewed same-gender marriage is crucial if we hope to make any progress on this issue.

A fifth question follows from the fourth one: *Should clergy be allowed to perform same-gender marriages?* The huge number of parachurch organizations and independent congregations in the world precludes any one-size-fits-all answer. But it is a question for every round-table conversation. On the one hand, given the covenant relationship among ordained clergy, I believe we

---

7. John Boswell, *Same Sex Unions in Premodern Europe* (New York: Harper Collins, 1994).

8. I have found the writing of Richard B. Hays and Richard John Neuhaus to be insightful in the critique of Boswell, but I know there are other voices to be heard on this particular point, from both those who agree and disagree with him. I have work to do here.

should be expected to uphold the current standards of our denomination. That is part of what it means to be in covenant community.[9]

But as same-gender marriages become increasingly legal, it is reasonable to assume that Christian same-gender couples will want to solemnize their relationship in the same way and to the same extent that male-female couples do. At that point, a judicatory could leave the decision of whether or not to perform a same-gender marriage to the discretion of the clergyperson, just as it does with respect to a male-female marriage. No clergyperson is required to marry anyone, but rather to make the decision prayerfully and carefully, given that the ceremony carries the recognition of the state and the blessing of the Christian faith with it.

A clergyperson should be expected to engage in pre-marital counseling with all couples. And he or she should be expected to insure that the marriage includes the elements I have previously described: sacredness (solemn pledges), monogamy, and fidelity. No Christian marriage should be performed if the couple is not committed to these principles. But if a couple profess the Christian faith and show evidence of seriousness with respect to the three ethical standards, the clergyperson should have the right to decide whether or not to perform a marriage ceremony. As with men and women, civil unions would be available for gay and lesbian persons not meeting this requirement.

A sixth question must be brought to the round-table: *What about ordaining gay or lesbian leaders to be clergy?* My own tradition, The United Methodist Church, has been open and charitable regarding gay, lesbian, bisexual, and transgendered persons as genuine Christians and members of the denomination.[10] But as I write these words, it continues the prohibition of

---

9. In my United Methodist tradition, we speak of ordained persons (deacons and elders) as members of an Order. There is no way to use this word theologically and historically without implying covenant accountability. Ordination vows place us *within* a covenant relationship, which among other things, requires us to live in congruence with the doctrines and discipline the denomination has put in place at any given time—and all the more so given we have said publicly (on more than one occasion) that we would do so. This does not mean the standards of the denomination cannot or should not change. It merely means that we have said we would obey the ones currently in place. If we cannot do this, we should do what Christians in other holy orders have done; surrender our membership and look for community elsewhere.

10. Unfortunately, this often gets lost in the debate. Everything gets "mixed up" into what appears to be a universal rejection of same-gender couples. If for nothing other than fairness, we must remember that the only line drawn in United Methodism is the continuing

"self-avowed, practicing homosexuals" from being ordained. The same holds true for many other denominations and parachurch organizations. Again, there are far too many expressions of institutional Christianity to propose a one-size-fits-all response. But I do believe that the principles and practices advocated in this book can provide a basis for any group approaching the issue of ordination.

Here we come back to the radical Christian position of celibacy in singleness and fidelity in marriage—for all clergy. As men and women go through the ordination process of their respective judicatory, the main concerns for theological substance, homiletical skill, leadership potential, and personal wholeness must continue to be in play. But perhaps we are at the time when the personal ethics of candidates must also be examined.[11] But whatever happens, it seems clear to me that the landscape for addressing this issue is changing in ways that we cannot deny or ignore.

Even the phrase "self-avowed, practicing homosexuals" was written with the prohibition essentially relating to single homosexual persons.[12] More than forty years ago, the matter of gay and lesbian marriage was not present in the church or society as it is today, so the current language is not adequate to take current reality into consideration. We will surely face in the future the approach of same-gender couples who are legally married, asking that the church respect their call to ordained ministry, and ordain them. We must not settle for being unprepared to deal with this, and accept no other approach

prohibition of "self-avowed, practicing homosexuals" from being ordained. But also for the sake of fairness, we must remember that the way the issue has been debated (even in United Methodism) has left many gay and lesbian Christians feeling stigmatized, even with respect to membership in the denomination.

11. I actually believe that the same-sex issue and its relationship to ordination has itself raised the need for this, as per the Christian prohibitions against sexual immorality for singles and adultery for married couples that we have already examined. Just as the theological and professional dimensions of ministry are subject to review, so now we must also evaluate the ethics and morality of ministerial candidates.

12. The United Methodist commitment to "celibacy in singleness and fidelity in marriage" has been the way the denomination has tried to create a mediating point in the issue. But fidelity in marriage was originally written against the backdrop of male-female marriage, not same-gender marriage. That has already changed, and will continue to do so, requiring us to revisit not only our theology but also what words we use to express it.

than to merely follow the culture. We must bring this question to the round table and address it in the context of the Christian faith.

A seventh question has arisen in the process of writing this chapter—one I would not have thought of on my own—one that my brothers and sisters in Christianity outside the United States have correctly put on the table: *How are we to deal with the consequences of a North American decision in other countries and cultures?* I am thinking here primarily of African and Asian Christians, and the fact that any perceived shift with respect to same-gender marriage will almost surely result in Christians being harassed, rejected, and perhaps even killed.

This is not unfounded exaggeration. It is a serious question. The way of love cannot ignore it, for in principle we seek no way forward that automatically jeopardizes any other Christian. If we do not deal with this question at the round table, we will have not only failed to invite all the significant persons to the conversation, we will have (once again) used some kind of cultural superiority to guide a decision that ends up inflicting pain and suffering somewhere else in the Body of Christ. This is not acceptable, and it is not a reflection of the kind of spirit that attends the round table or the way of love.

At the very least, it seems to me that we would have to make it crystal clear that the decision regarding same-gender marriage would be limited to the United States or other places where it would be adopted. At this point in time, I cannot see how we could expect a pro-gay position to be required everywhere in the world. This obviously makes our round-table conversation much more complicated. But the issue of universal application cannot be ignored.

All we can do in a book like this is open some doors and try to walk through them with new eyes and a sensitive spirit. But when we truly open doors, we let in air from the outside—air that can refresh the stagnant air that has developed when we have been shut up in our respective war rooms.

I do not know of any concept that is more radical or more needed today than that of the round table. It embodies the way of love in both principle and practice. It is a radical departure from the way we most often address critical issues by limiting our interaction with those who already agree with us, stigmatizing almost immediately others as wrong and even unchristian. The round table declares a decisive "No" to that approach. The questions I am left with as I bring this chapter to a close is this: "Do we have the courage to gather at the round table—for the sake of the Bride?"[13]

---

13. I believe the round-table approach also challenges a majority-rule approach, or one that is driven by Robert's Rules of Order. The issues we face are too formidable to simply assume that 51 percent of a group holds 100 percent of the truth. And even more, we will be a stronger church when we can move forward by consensus. That is what the round table has the potential to achieve. In principle, every group has something to contribute. The round table provides a process for discerning what that is, and then utilizing it for the advance of a new and larger truth.

Sixteen

Into the Future

Long ago, Socrates said, "Strong minds discuss ideas, average minds discuss events, weak minds discuss people." From the outset of this book, I have been writing out of the conviction that there are *strong minds* in the Body of Christ—people who are weary of replaying the old tapes and warming up the old arguments—people who believe that God is waiting to bless us, if we use our strong minds in the way Socrates describes them.

But my conviction is not rooted in Greek philosophy; it is based on the revelation of scripture and the witness of tradition over four thousand years—a witness that shows both the courage and willingness of Jews and Christians to face formidable challenges with faith, and one that confirms God's willingness to lead them to new discoveries. Every age in church history that can be described as one of reform or renewal has found men and women stepping up to the plate with the holy mix of courage and humility, believing that a way forward is possible. By risking caricature and shunning, they have nevertheless worked to bring to pass a vision that burned in their hearts.

I do not need to repeat what is obvious, but I will do so for the sake of emphasis: I believe we have entered a time such as this. It is a time to release ourselves from the grip of decades-old controversy, which (even during the time of writing this book) has evidenced that things are not really getting better when the old arguments about same-gender relationships are brought out and used. It is a time when the old default button of schism (even called "an amiable separation") is thought to be the best we can come up with. But one of my major points in this book is that this kind of thinking is driven, in part, by our unwillingness to gather at the round table, where some other option might be given to us by the Holy Spirit.

To say it another way, the old processes have patterned us toward negativity and divisiveness. The way of love does not accept these attitudes and actions as the only options that we have. At least we can hope for this as we move into the future, and that is what I want to write about in this chapter. As with the previous chapters, I want to look at a few factors which I believe God could use to lead us to a better place. I will identify them individually, but the power and potential I see in them is in their being combined into a singular vision that can transform us all—somewhat like the way the concentration of light beams by a magnifying glass produces fire. Some may see this as naiveté, but I see it as faith: "the reality of what we hope for, the proof of what we don't see" (Heb 11:1).

It begins in mutual conviction—the conviction that we can do better. Rather than polishing the patina of our particular points of view, we come realizing that no single person or group has the truth; indeed, that truth is always larger than a single vantage point can provide. We come believing that everyone at the table is a person who wants the best and is prepared to present his or her best case toward that end. In other words, we come to the table with hope.

Like so many others, I have been deeply moved by Pope Francis's immediate commitment to the way of hope. He has made it the hallmark of his papacy so far. In one of his first papal homilies he said,

> Please do not let yourselves be robbed of hope! Do not let hope be stolen! The hope that Jesus gives us.[1]

With all my heart I believe that Pope Francis is the most visible sign of the new thing God wants to do in the church and world today. The Pope's vision and voice is one all Christians should attend to, and then in our respective contexts work to emulate. This Christian leader has looked at the condi-

---

1. Homily of March 3, 2013 (Copyright by the Liberia Editrice Vaticana).

tion of the church and the world, and through the lens of hope has said, we can do better.

The way forward continues through mutual confession. We move forward on the basis of radical humility, another major point in this book. In its absence we turn the legitimate differentiation of dualistic thinking into divisiveness that emerges when we make our differences hierarchical. But when we begin our movement forward with the conviction that all have sinned, and that there is no righteous person—not even one, we find ourselves in a much different atmosphere. I believe it is one that God is waiting to bless in ways beyond what we can ask or imagine. The atmosphere of humility levels what is too often a slanted playing field. This too is part of hope, because we initiate and maintain our relationships with each other on the basis of radical grace—the only thing that saves any of us.

Thirdly, we move forward by mutual conversation. Simply put, we keep talking. We do so because of our first conviction that progress is possible. But we do so realizing that movement is almost always incremental—little by little. Conversation is the means through which we find the small achievements and little advances. We cannot predict when they will come, or how. But we keep talking in the belief that time and time again we will find ourselves saying, "Yes, I see that! That makes sense. This is a better way." And when we experience such Spirit-inspired moments, we will move together to a better place.

I believe that staying together is a sacred act—a holy experience. As I have said before, we have become patterned to disagree and divide. But the witness in the Trinity is to unite and to be one. Human oneness will never match divine unity, but God's unified nature and God's action to redeem all things in and through Christ is the model for our attitudes and actions. Rather than starting with the assumption that the best we can do is to have some kind of amiable separation, we say instead, "We will not separate. We will stay together in prayer, in conversation, and in action—believing that this kind of spiritual tenacity will create some kind of forward progress."

Fourthly, we move forward through mutual cooperation. I experienced the power of this principle in 2001 a few days after the tragedy of 9-11. In the Orlando area, Muslim girls were being bullied in the public schools. Their holy coverings were pulled off, and sacred items were stolen from them. They were harassed on the bus to and from school, and in the hallways between classes. In addition, a Muslim family had its rear window shot out on the freeway, narrowly missing a child riding in the back seat.

The Florida Council of Churches said, in effect, "enough is enough." The leader of the Council created a round table. Out of the blue, I received a call from him, asking me to be one of the three Protestants at the table. We were joined there by Roman and Orthodox Christians, and by Jewish, Hindu, Sikh, Buddhist, and Muslim leaders. Members of the educational and public safety communities also sat at the table.

We began with the conviction that things could be better, indeed, had to become better in order to check the downward spiral of tension and violence in the Orlando area. We began each of our meetings with prayer—prayer to the one God who does not desire any of God's children to be bullied or shot at. We sensed that God was with us, and we tried to honor that through the ways we related to each other.

Somewhere in this round-table process, I received a phone call from a person who challenged my commitment to Christ, telling me that no one should meet with "the Muslim infidels." I asked the caller if he was familiar with E. Stanley Jones. He said that he knew Brother Stanley's writings well. So I replied, "I am sure you know about his Round Table concept, and how Stanley Jones use it in his missionary ministry." At that moment, the phone fell silent. Total silence. And after about five seconds, I heard the little click indicating that the caller had hung up. He had nothing more to say. He knew what I was driving at.

I continued at the Orlando round table, and little-by-little God led our group. We found ways to take our concern back to our respective faith communities, interpreting the situation with our respective theologies and commitments. The local media carried reports of our work, providing the larger metropolitan area with the opportunity to think about ways to maintain civility in a time of tension.

And, thanks be to God, things did improve. God honored the cries of the people and the tensions declined. As we came to the time when we sensed we had essentially achieved the goal that brought us together in the first place, one member said, "Should we not find some way to thank God for hearing our prayers and honoring our work?" Of course, we agreed. And with a bit more conversation and planning, God led us to conduct a joint prayer service in one of the large high-school auditoriums. There, hundreds of Orlando-area residents gathered to celebrate the reduction in tension and to thank God for bringing us to a better place.

I have gone to some lengths to report this real-life experience, because it is Exhibit A for the conviction that progress is possible. All of the principles that I have previously described came together in the Orlando round table. And best of all, God was with us! It is because of this experience, and a few others like it, that I believe there is a level of mutual cooperation possible—a level that God will bless.[2]

Before I leave this fourth point, I want to extract another principle from it—the principle of locality. Simply put, things can get done sooner and better when we do them close to home. The wheels of institutional change turn slowly, as our forty-year debate about same-gender relationships in The United Methodist Church reveals. And, in some cases, the complexities of change at the denominational level are so many and varied as to make the effort exhausting.

But at the local level, things can happen. The Orlando-area round table proved it. None of us consulted our respective judicatory. We did not ask them for permission or guidance. But neither did we violate any of their prohibitions. We acted on the basis of religious conscience. We gathered as men and women charged by God with the responsibility to be maintainers of spiritual welfare in the city. We brought our faith traditions with us, making use of them for wisdom. But we operated *locally*, applying the generic insights of our faith to the specific situation we were facing. God taught me, as never before, the powerful lesson of *locality* through this experience. As you face challenging issues in general in your community, and as you face the specific issue of same-gender marriage, I believe the principle of mutual cooperation is one God will use to enable you to find a way forward.

---

2. As I write these words, I have just learned about a cooperative effort between gay and straight churches in Portland, Oregon. It is called "City Serve." Christians are uniting there in new ways and finding that their disagreements are not higher than their vision. I invite you to learn more about this kind of cooperation, even as I intend to do so myself.

Finally, the way forward is enabled by a mutual covenant. This means there are no double standards. Everyone lives by and is accountable to common values. I find the Christian precedent for this in the Jerusalem Council, as the first Christians debated how Gentiles were to be accepted into what had previously been a community almost entirely made up of converted Jews. It is clear that critical differences of opinion existed in the original fellowship. And it is clear that everyone was free to express his or her opinion. But when the matter was finally resolved, the newly formed Jew/Gentile Christian community lived by one standard—a standard which brought both an honored behavior and a means to live with accountability.[3]

I see this same principle at work in the production of the classic creeds of Christianity. A cursory look at them reveals how many different ways things could have gone on almost every point that is affirmed in one or more of them. But amazingly (and I believe providentially), the Christian community wrote affirmations of faith for the larger Body of Christ, and then made them the basis of defining Christian doctrine and life together.

We are such an individualized and privatized culture in the United States that we hardly know how to make and keep a mutual covenant. But we have been given the heritage and the examples of such activity. We must use this principle in moving forward with respect to any divisive issue, including same-gender marriage. Gathering together what I have said previously, I make the modest proposal that the covenant for human sexuality continues to be rooted in celibate singleness and marital fidelity. This covenant establishes the Christian resistance to sexual immorality and adultery, and it provides the basis for all people to agree to be held accountable for their actions.

Here is precisely why I have maintained throughout this book that the way of love—the third way, the way forward—is not soft on sin. In fact, given the pluralistic nature of North American society, I believe such a covenant would actually increase morality and increase a life together that is genuine. Simply put, I would not be permitted to violate this Rule of Life without

---

3. I find it interesting and significant that within the decision reached by the Jerusalem Council, the prohibition against sexual immorality was included (Acts 15:29), another indication that it is possible to maintain the ethical standard while at the same time forging a third way. But even here it should not escape our attention that celibacy in singleness and fidelity in marriage was not compromised.

consequence. Instead, the covenant produced by the round-table community would be enforced, and that by common consent.

I say this with respect to the same-sex issue, because I do not know a single straight person or gay or lesbian person who is in favor of sexual immorality or adultery. So why would we not actually *want* the church to hold us accountable along these lines? I realize this universal affirmation rests upon the controversial assumption that the recognition of same-sex marriage actually elevates the status of the Christian ethic by making it applicable to everyone. This is one place where we need round-table conversation.

But however we deal with this, we do not have to assume that holding single persons to celibacy, whether they are straight, lesbian, or gay, diminishes human sexuality. And we do not have to assume that heterosexual marriage is diminished if we allow same-sex marriage. Rather, it is possible to envision that everyone is enriched as Christianity takes a clear stand against sexual immorality and adultery, no matter who the person or couple may be. Obviously, there is much disagreement here, and we have a ton of work to do in order to see if it is possible. But the vision is there.

I return for a moment to the two Christians named at the beginning of the book: E. Stanley Jones and Martin Luther King, Jr. As I continue to read about their lives and their ministries—and as I read their own writings—I am convinced that they saw their challenges in much the same light as we see the current controversy about same-sex marriage.

E. Stanley Jones saw an India divided by cultural ideology and religious differences—a country splintered, and with almost no energy for coming back together. Animosity and anger were the societal fuel more than love. But with a theology of love, rooted in the Trinity in general and the incarnation of Jesus in particular, Jones moved with humility and courage to confront the disintegration of a land he believed God had called him to serve in Jesus' name.

Similarly, Martin Luther King Jr. saw the United States divided in a violent and death-dealing racism—a nation splintered and with almost no energy for coming back together. Animosity and anger were the societal fuel more than love. But with a theology of love, rooted in the Judeo-Christian tradition, King moved with what he called "the strength to love"—the same kind of humility and courage that he had found in Jones and in Jones's biography of Gandhi. He believed that God had called him to serve the United States this way, in Jesus' Name.

And that is where I stand, coming out of Lent 2014 with the experiences it provided me. I believe the way of love is the way forward. As with Jones and King (and others before and after them), I do not believe there will be a complete resolution to all the issues that divide us. India remains divided in old and new ways more than a hundred years after Jones first set foot there. And the United States still finds individual and corporate racism present, after more than fifty years since King came upon the scene. The point here is simply that a fallen-world system calls for never-ending vigil and unceasing action. We can never rest in our efforts to achieve what we believe is best.

But the vigil and action have to be in relation to some kind of center point; otherwise, we will try to find on the circumference what only God can provide at the center. Coming out of my experience in Lent 2014, I am convinced that our time is ripe for a renewal of the way of love. I am convinced that it is the way forward—for the sake of the Bride.

Seventeen

The Power of Love

When Pope Francis chose the design of the papal cross that he wears each day around his neck, he did not choose a traditional crucifix. He chose a cross with the Good Shepherd on it—Jesus carrying the one lost sheep on his shoulders, the lost sheep he has found, redeemed, and returned to the fold. Behind him is what we can easily imagine are the other ninety-nine sheep, following Jesus as he leads them *all* home.

Pope Francis chose this design based upon Luke 15:3-7, where the redemptive effort of Christ is based upon our Lord's hope that the one lost sheep can be found, and based upon the joy that erupts when it happens! Consequently, Pope Francis has made the united elements of hope and joy the hallmarks of his papacy. And he is now in the process of enacting personal pronouncements and collective councils to move both the church and society into a new day.[1]

During Lent of 2014, Pope Francis's cross became the metaphor for me—the metaphor of mercy and the metaphor of ministry. It is the metaphor of mercy because it is the picture of radical grace—grace that can find us when we are lost and carry us home. It is the metaphor of mercy because

---

1. See Pope Francis's book *The Church of Mercy* (Loyola University Press, 2014).

things look different when we are being *carried*, when we admit we cannot make it without the Risen Christ taking us where we need to go.

It is also the metaphor of ministry because in the example of Christ, we find our example. The sheep is sought for, found, and returned home solely on the basis that it is lost. How it got lost is immaterial. There is no assessment of the sheep's goodness or badness. All we see in Luke's Gospel and on the pope's cross is a Good Shepherd bringing the sheep home.

The challenge of the gospel, and the challenge I have tried to represent in this book, is the necessity of seeing ourselves (all of us) as being carried by Christ. It is the eschatological vision that at the Day of Christ Jesus "everyone in heaven, on earth, and under the earth might bow and every tongue confess that Jesus Christ is Lord, to the glory of God the Father" (Phil 2:10). If our knees are bowed, we are not standing—that is the way of grace—and no one is left standing when the way of Christ prevails. And if our knees are bowed, no one is walking—and that is the way of love—we are all carried along by power that is not ours. And if with our bowed knees, all one hundred sheep "confess that Jesus Christ is Lord," the world may be on the verge of seeing a form of Christianity that is so often unseen when "churchianity" prevails.

When I began this book, it was the result of my experience in Lent 2014. But as I have continued to reflect upon that experience, and to write about it, I now realize it is part of my larger Christian journey—a journey which now encompasses more than fifty years. Surprisingly, and happily, I am finding my experience with the way of love to be a strengthening of my Christian orthodoxy, not a weakening of it. I have a fresh vision of the power of scripture as I move into the future—a vision given me in the earliest days of my Christian experience when I memorized, "For God so loved the world that he gave his only begotten Son, that whosoever believeth in him, should not perish, but have everlasting life" (John 3:16 KJV). That verse now shines with new brightness when I pause over the words "love" and "whosoever"—and all because of who God is, and the gift of salvation given to us in Jesus.

I have a fresh vision of the power of tradition as I revisit the lives of the saints—men and women who looked at their respective periods of history with as much concern as we do, and with the faith to believe that God could lead that world to a better place. They lived with the fruit of the Spirit and the practice of non-judgment empowering and guiding them. And even though none of them achieved 100 percent of what they might have hoped for, they were blessed by God, who enabled them to achieve more than they could ask or imagine.

Within this great cloud of witnesses, I am encouraged by the courageous reformers (some noted in Heb 11), who did not think their own lives worth protecting, for the sake of the larger reality that the gospel held out. They dared to believe that new ways could be found, new paths forged, new attitudes inspired, and better outcomes achieved. They did not allow subcategories to define them (including sexual orientation), but rather sought to keep the two great commandments central, as God has intended all along.

And through it all, I have found my commitment to covenant living strengthened. I have seen the destructive consequences of actions that violate the community. And while I can see in church history (ancient and modern) acts of conscience that people felt compelled to do, I still see that a certain spirit of unity and life together is always lost, especially when covenant members try to be bold but still be institutionally protected at the same time. Instead of this, I see that the way of love calls for a round-table discussion—a holy conferencing that leads to a statement of commitment and a renewal of covenant. Everyone would then be expected to abide by it. My college sociology major tells me that anything other than this keeps institutions in chaos.[2]

But within the boundaries of orthodox Christian faith, and within the boundaries of historic Christian ethics, I also believe that life together in covenant community and accountability calls for us to always resist sexual immorality and adultery. These are prohibitions God has put in place in both Testaments, and which have continued to be enforced in tradition. They are not up for grabs in the current debate. All human beings, made in the image of God (regardless of sexual orientation) must agree not to act in ways that defile sexuality by either of these sins. No one is exempt.

---

2. In this regard, I can only speak for myself. But I can tell you that this view would mean that if, under current United Methodist standards, I presided at a same-gender wedding, I would immediately thereafter surrender my credentials as an elder in The United Methodist Church. I would affirm the bonds of marriage, but do so with a follow-up action that did not break the bond of the covenant I was asked to make several times in my ordination process as an elder in The United Methodist Church.

But within the covenant that holds us accountable, I believe the way of love offers us hope. Here, I have had to distinguish between arriving at a final solution and making some progress. The way I have proposed maintains the biblical and historical resistance to sexual immorality and adultery. It holds firm the Christian ethic of celibacy in singleness and fidelity in marriage. The new way is that it proposes this as an ethic for male-female couples and same-sex couples. It makes this way accessible to all human beings. I believe this is a level of covenant, commitment, concord, and community that the current debate has failed to find. In that sense, I see it as a way forward.

This conviction is beyond the ability of any single person to create apart from the larger church. But it is not beyond the ability of the church itself, not only to envision it but also to work along new lines to see how it might become real. It means that we might at least try to turn our swords into ploughshares and our spears into pruning hooks, and see what happens after that. I believe God is waiting for us to do this. And I believe we would be blessed somehow if we did it.

In proposing this pathway, I am aware of the limitations of what I have written in this book. Some will ask, "Why did you leave that out?"—or—"Why didn't you address this?" Some will see my interpretation of the way of love as inadequate. And some may never be able to view what I have written as "Christian." But such is the incomplete nature of a single vantage point, and the risk in trying to advocate a better way. Every position is incomplete; every camp is inadequate.

The insufficiencies are present because I am insufficient. I need to recommit myself to centering my life in the two great commandments. I need to allow the fruit of the Spirit to be reignited in me. I need to practice the way of non-judgment. I need the round table. I need to be more Christlike. I need everything I have proposed in this book, and more. And for it to happen, I need grace!

The point of this book is simply that if the new way could become reality, I believe God would do a new thing in our midst. I can only say with E. Stanley Jones, "I am a Christian under construction"—and—with Martin Luther King Jr., "I have decided to stick to love...hate is too great a burden to bear." I have come to the place where I am unwilling to settle for anything less than the way of love—for the sake of the Bride.

About the Author

Steve Harper taught spiritual formation and Wesley studies to Christian divinity students for more than thirty years. He is a native of Texas, graduating in 1966 from Haskell High School and McMurry University in Abilene in 1970. He received his MDiv from Asbury Theological Seminary in 1973, and the PhD in Wesley studies from Duke University in 1981.

Across the years, Dr. Harper's ministries have included youth minister, evangelist, pastor, professor, and seminary administrator. He and his wife Jeannie oversaw A Foundation for Theological Education, and they cofounded Shepherd's Care, a ministry to ministers. Steve served as dean of the chapel and director of the Pathways Initiative at The Upper Room in Nashville.

Steve Harper received his license to preach in The Methodist Church in 1965, became a deacon in The United Methodist Church in 1971 and an elder in 1974. He has held membership in the Northwest Texas Annual Conference and the Florida Annual Conference.

Steve has authored sixteen books, coauthored another thirteen, and written numerous articles. He speaks frequently in local churches, conferences, and retreats. He and Jeannie have been married since 1970. They are the parents of two children, and they have three grandchildren.

Made in the USA
San Bernardino, CA
09 March 2015